LOVE IN A BOX

THE INSPIRING STORY OF DAVE COOKE AND
Operation Christmas Child®

Written by
Emma Carswell

First published in 2001 by Paternoster Lifestyle

07 06 05 04 03 02 01   7 6 5 4 3 2 1

Paternoster Lifestyle is an imprint of Paternoster Publishing, PO Box 300, Carlisle, Cumbria, CA3 0QS, UK
and Paternoster Publishing USA, PO Box 1047, Waynesboro, GA 30830-2047.
www.paternoster-publishing.com

Operation Christmas Child is a registered trademark of Samaritan's Purse, a charitable nonprofit organisation,
PO Box 3000, Boone, North Carolina 28607, United States of America.

British Library Cataloguing in Publication Data

A catalogue record for this book is available from the British Library.

ISBN 1-85078-366-7

Designed by Diane Bainbridge

Printed in Great Britain by Bath Press

LOVE IN A BOX
Operation Christmas Child®

Contents

Emma Carswell

Acknowledgements

My thanks must first go to Les Lever, who has faithfully supported Operation Christmas Child from the very beginning and who gave hours of work to this project. In different ways his humour and brilliant skills as a journalist made this book happen. Thanks, too, to Anthea Fryatt, who transcribed tape after tape and made my task so much easier.

To editor, Carol Grugeon, thanks for doing such a super job. Stephen King said, 'To write is human, to edit is divine' - I couldn't agree more. Designer Diane Bainbridge has shone - again! On a personal note, both Carol and Diane have been great friends and encouragers; it has been great to work with them on this project.

The staff at the Operation Christmas Child offices in Wrexham helped with the painstaking process of sourcing photographs, cuttings and reports. I also owe a big thank you to all the photographers and journalists who have covered Operation Christmas Child over the years - some of whom I've enjoyed the company of on trips and others who did so much of the groundwork for this book, but whom I've never met.

To the generous sponsors of this book who have made it possible for each book sold to provide a donation to help meet the needs of suffering children: thank you to each one of you.

Carol Pope of the University of Dundee and Mark Finnie at Paternoster Publishing have both been great mentors from whom I've learnt much. I'm grateful to both of them for the wealth of opportunities they've given me.

Finally to two great families - the Cookes and the Carswells. Writing this book has made me realise what an immense privilege it is to grow up surrounded by a loving family. In both cases, a very patient and praying woman supports four children and a husband who is away a lot, living a very unusual life for God! Thanks to each one of you for being incredibly tolerant and supportive.

Emma Carswell

Rick Parry

Foreword

Operation Christmas Child captured my attention for a number of reasons. Firstly, I was impressed with Dave Cooke's fairly apparent energy and dedication to the cause. Secondly, like all of the best ideas it has a terrific simplicity. You can't help thinking: 'Wow, why didn't I think of that?' Thirdly, there's the fact that each child who fills a shoebox almost feels they have a one-to-one relationship with the recipient. Fourthly, it is very clear that every shoe box goes to a child, not just X% of a donation. And finally, my own children, like so many others, had already enjoyed being involved in the programme.

Football clubs have enormous influence, especially in the lives of kids, and this is something that must never be taken for granted. The medium of top football is a great leveller and fantastic for people who have very little. Anyone can take part in the game, and as clubs we have a responsibility to use the power and privileges in a positive way. The involvement of professional footballers in the coaching programmes of Operation Christmas Child is one thing we can do. It has real benefits for the club too - when our players met children from the orphanages in Romania it helped them to realise that there are indeed things that are far more important than football.

I was both surprised and honoured when Dave asked me to write the Foreword for 'Love in a Box'. There are certainly others who would be far better qualified - who have done much more than I ever will. However, it is a pleasure to commend this book to you. Dave Cooke has a totally unshakable dedication to what he's doing but, as you'll see, he's a very ordinary guy...and a very average goalkeeper! I hope you'll not only be interested in reading about Dave, but that you too will be inspired to give something back - to reach out to people in need.

Rick Parry

Chief Executive, Liverpool Football Club

Risks

To laugh is to risk appearing the fool.

To weep is to risk appearing sentimental.

To reach out to another is to risk involvement.

To expose feelings is to risk exposing your true self.

To place your ideas and dreams before a crowd is to risk their loss.

To love is to risk not being loved in return.

To live is to risk dying.

To try is to risk failure.

But risks must be taken because the greatest hazard in life is to risk nothing.

The person who risks nothing, has nothing and is nothing.

He may avoid suffering and sorrow, but he cannot learn, feel, change, grow or live.

Chained only by his certitudes, he is a slave; he has forfeited his freedom.

Only a person who risks is free.

Author Unknown

Introduction

Arriving at Liverpool Airport ready to board the Antonov aircraft to Armenia, I never imagined that three years later I would be writing the story of how Operation Christmas Child began. I still think those ten days were the best of my life. My eyes were opened to a world that I'd been aware of, but had no idea could affect me so immensely.

I saw the difference that Operation Christmas Child makes to little children whose lives have been torn apart through war, poverty, political oppression, and natural disaster. I held children in my arms who had been starved of love, happiness and the security of a home and family. Operation Christmas Child is in the business of bringing hope and love to these children by telling them that someone, somewhere cares.

It has been a wonderful privilege to work on this project and to get to know Dave Cooke more. He is an incredible guy, aware of his own failings, but also confident that God is able to use him just as he is, to demonstrate God's love to others.

When we were talking about writing this book I remember Dave saying, 'I'm not into empire building. This isn't about Dave Cooke. It's about God getting hold of a project and working through people.' My prayer is that as you read this story and take in the images, that you will be inspired to see what God could do through you too, if you are willing to let Him.

Emma Carswell, Summer 2001

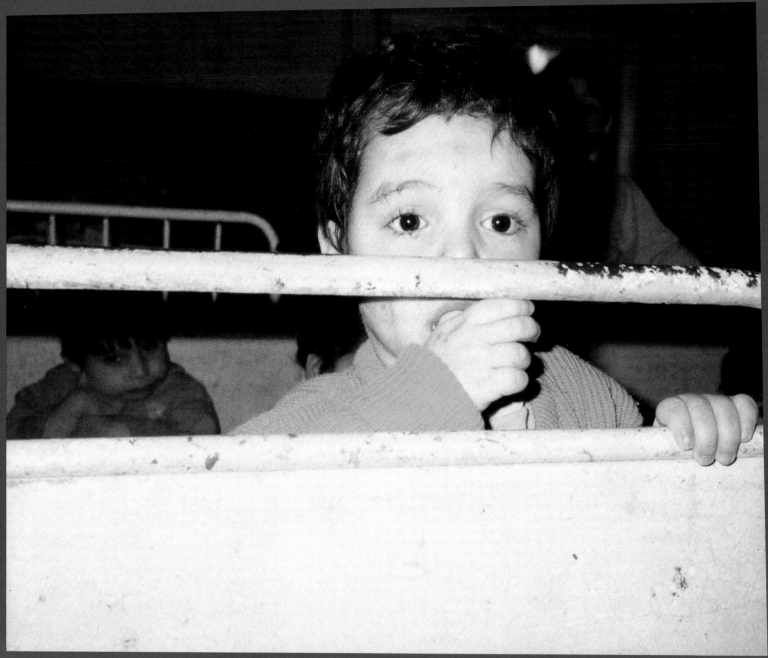

From Wrexham to Romania

Nothing could have prepared the Operation Christmas Child team for the horror that awaited them when they arrived at the first orphanage. Driving through impoverished peasant farms and villages, the landscape threw them back a couple of generations. The gates of the orphanage were obstructed by a crowd of gypsies, desperate to get their hands on the supplies so they could sell them on. Determined to reach the children, the volunteers climbed out of the trucks, filled their arms with shoe boxes and pushed their way into the muddy grey courtyard. As they looked up, they saw a huddle of gaunt-faced children staring blankly at them through a barred window ahead.

It was December 1990 and a long way from the Christmas rush of Wrexham which the team had left a few days earlier: the contrast could not have been starker. It had only been a few weeks since the first bleak pictures of the children of Romania had been seen in the West. As the shops began to make space for Christmas decorations, and brightly-coloured lights were strung across the high streets, television screens were presenting a much bleaker prospect for these children. Images of the oppressive orphanages of the Ceausescu regime left very few Britons unmoved by the cruelty and injustice.

Yet, while most of us felt powerless to help, one man in the Welsh border town of Wrexham wasn't prepared to sit and watch their plight from the comfort of his home. Dave Cooke was always one to befriend the downtrodden and to speak up for those who cannot or dare not. He felt the urge to go to Romania himself, to give what he had to those who had nothing.

'It tells us in the Bible that we have got to do something practical, not just spout words. I thought this is where I could offer my services and went about setting up a little committee to organise Operation Christmas Child.'

Dave Cooke

In 1990, Western Europe was stunned to see pictures of Romanian orphans struggling in desperate conditions. Images and reports spoke of children living in cramped, squalid hospitals with few medical experts and supplies. Babies were reportedly dying of AIDS, often contracted through infected needles in the hospitals. Little children were strapped to chairs for minor operations, such as having their tonsils removed, because of the lack of anaesthetics. In the orphanages, others were condemned to life without play, love and care during the harsh Ceausescu regime.

From the outset of their marriage, Dave and Gill Cooke had made a habit of reading the Bible and praying together. As committed Christians, their relationship with God was right at the centre of their lives, and they regularly asked Him for direction. Dave couldn't get the television images out of his head, and began to wonder if this was God prompting him to do something new for Him.

A meal with friends John and Carol Roberts had been in the diary for some time, but the timing was perfect. As they ate, the conversation naturally turned to the pictures of the little Romanian kids who had nothing and were being cruely treated. Knowing Dave to be impulsive, it was little surprise to everyone when he turned to John and asked, 'Do you fancy driving a truck full of supplies to Romania with me?'

Some months earlier Dave had heard a man speak about his work taking aid into Poland and had thought at the time that this was something he could do. The overwhelming situation in Romania presented him with an opportunity that he could turn into a reality. The adventure had begun.

First thing next morning Dave proposed the idea to his brother Paul and Dai Hughes, a friend with whom he played football. Both agreed to be part of a basic committee which would decide where to go from there. Not appreciating the power of the media, Dave had no idea at this stage that Dai's employers, local radio station Marcher Sound, would take this from being one man's personal vision to a campaign that would capture the heart of the town of Wrexham and beyond.

Looking back, Dave is quick to acknowledge he couldn't have done it on his own: 'Right from the beginning God provided top professionals - God-fearing people who rallied around us and made things happen.' Godfrey Williams was one of these provisions. As Managing Director of Marcher Sound, he immediately caught the vision, jumping at an opportunity to respond to the massive problems in Romania. Between the wholehearted support of the radio station and the local newspaper, The Wrexham Mail, they found themselves in the heart of a highly effective PR machine. From day one, things began to happen, and the funds and supplies started pouring in.

Christmas was approaching and as the men sat chatting one day, Dave's eight-year-old daughter, Naomi, was drawing a crude star. When they saw it, they picked up the paper and excitedly agreed that that would be their logo. It had the duel effect of suggesting the birth of Christ and the involvement of children. All they needed now was a name - something to instantly identify the campaign. They definitely wanted the word 'child' in the name, and it was Christmas, so what about 'Operation Christmas Child'? Everyone was agreed - and Operation Christmas Child was born.

Over the next few weeks nobody in Wrexham had the opportunity to miss the Operation Christmas Child logo: the stars were found everywhere. One bright spark pre-empted the Red Nose appeal and made hundreds of plastic Operation Christmas Child stars for car bonnets. These and matching stickers were to raise thousands of pounds for the campaign.

Operation Christmas Child

> '**I've never been one to do things by halves. If it went pear-shaped I'd blow it big style, not in a small way. However, if I did anything in marketing or sales or organising in the window company, it was always done professionally. So to see Operation Christmas Child get off to the start it did was completely absorbing. It was hard to take it all in.**'
>
> Dave Cooke

Marcher Sound's on-air launch of its Christmas charity project could not have gone better. Presenters described how Romanians had been brutalised by the ruthless dictator Nicolae Ceausescu. They explained how it had been government policy to force women to bear at least four children, regardless of whether they had any means of bringing them up.

This was Operation Christmas Child's first public request for help. Once off-air, everyone in the studio waited anxiously for a reaction from the listeners. 'Suddenly all the office phones lit up like Christmas trees,' Dai Hughes recalled. People rang from all over the area: medical staff from Wrexham, Runcorn, Preston and Manchester; physiotherapists from Liverpool; housewives from Chester and Shrewsbury - all offering their help and services. It had provoked an emotional response, and many of the callers were in tears.

Marcher's phone system quickly became jammed and it stayed that way. The public response was snowballing before their eyes. Marcher kept pounding out the story, with Dave joining them on-air to explain the goals of Operation Christmas Child. He announced a list of the goods desperately needed in Romania and what would be required to get them there, asking people for 'sacrificial giving'.

A moving account of the Romanians' plight by Wrexham Mail's Chief Reporter Cath Steward widened the impact of the story still further. Within hours, the Marcher studios were swamped with nappies, children's shoes, toys, soap, saucepans, food parcels, bandages, blankets - the list was endless!

What had started as a snowball was quickly turning into an avalanche! Operation Christmas Child desperately needed help as the idea conceived in Dave's front room was now a campaign that was dominating the region. Marcher decided to set up a reception area in its main office where the public could deliver all their gifts.

Volunteers were quick to offer their help. Wives Jayne Cooke, Carol Roberts and Margaret Peet stepped in to perform innumerable miracles of organisation to restore order out of the chaos in Marcher's foyer.

The involvement of Steve Edmunds, a man with vast experience in dealing with hospitals and drug companies, proved to be a huge asset. Launching a personal mission to gather enough equipment to satisfy all the hospitals in Romania, he began by knocking on doors at his own medical supplies company and Wrexham Maelor Hospital. The response from both was phenomenal, so from there he set off to northern England looking for further help.

Ton after ton of medical equipment started arriving in Wrexham, from defibrillators to portable X-ray machines and from wheelchairs to incubators - even vans full of bandages, dressings, mattresses and crutches. Before long over £500,000 worth of medical equipment was waiting to be delivered to Romania. The original plan to take two trucks was looking a little small scale; to carry all the aid they were now looking at ten lorries.

Operation Christmas Child was outgrowing the foyer at Marcher Sound and there was a desperate need for a warehouse. Dave picked up the phone, dialled the Welsh Development Agency and asked if they could help out by providing a warehouse. In fact, he wasn't just asking for any warehouse: 'We need 25,000 sq. ft. - and I could really do with the one next door to where I work!' The WDA came back with a firm yes, so Operation Christmas Child found themselves with the warehouse of their choice, enabling Dave to easily manage distributions and deliveries.

Margaret Peet & Helen Williamson answer the phones at Operation Christmas Child's makeshift office in the Marcher Sound Foyer

'Suddenly all the office phones lit up like Christmas trees'

Dai Hughes

Dave and Paul Cooke's sister, Jan, who also lived in the Wrexham area, had the brilliant idea of asking every child to wrap a shoe box in Christmas paper and fill it with things another child would enjoy - like a real stocking in a box. The idea was that each shoe box would be sealed with a message of love in the form of a Christmas card or a letter.

Immediately thousands of shoe boxes started to pour in. The idea was simple, personal and fun - and children jumped at it. Such was the response that a van was put to full-time use, visiting schools on a daily basis to collect the thousands of shoe boxes.

> The community spirit in the Wrexham area was incredible. Everyone was aware of the campaign and eager to help in any way they could. Five women even took begging bowls round their street and collected a staggering £750, such was the genuine desire to give.

A large Wrexham-based chemical company expressed interest in giving a donation of £5,000. They sent a representative from their PR agency to meet Dave and Dai to find out more. With no office of their own, the guys agreed to meet in the foyer of Marcher Sound.

The PR executive was sceptical to say the least. He reeled off questions, 'Why should we give you £5,000?; Who are you?; You've no experience - what will you do with the money?' As they sat there trying to break through the obvious lack of feeling and compassion, two little girls walked through the glass doors.

Wearing wellies that came up over their knees, they clearly weren't well off. But, runny noses and all, they ran towards Dave and presented their bucket with a few coins in the bottom. As they looked up at him they explained, 'Dave, we want you to take this to the poor children of Romania.'

The PR executive's expression said it all. It had blown him away. It's not unlike the Bible story where Jesus fed five thousand people because a little boy gave all he had. He handed over just five loaves and two fishes; these little girls gave the few coins they had, but this simple yet heartfelt donation made such an impact that the PR agency pushed through the gift of £5,000.

For Dave, it was God's seal of approval on what was to be the most substantial donation received in that first year: 'It was almost as if He was saying, "You're going the right way; I'm with you."'

An elderly blind lady phoned the Operation Christmas Child desk to say she had some money to donate to the appeal, but was not able to address an envelope to send in the money. One of the campaign volunteers went to her house and she handed over £20 - plus £1 for petrol!

On the day of the send off, the Daily Star awarded the people of Wrexham its coveted 'Golden Star Award'. Presented in honour of the town's achievement of raising a staggering £600,000 in cash and aid in just seven weeks to help the suffering Romanian orphans, the Daily Star summed up the effort in a simple message - 'Well done wonderful Wrexham'.

'Every member of the Wrexham community should feel proud of the part they have played in this wonderful gesture. Their concern and caring for people in need so far away is a tremendous example to us all. They have shown that there are no barriers when it comes to helping people less fortunate than ourselves. I salute every one of them.'

Brian Hitchen,
Editor, Daily Star, December 1990

Dave Cooke, Godfrey Williams (Director MFM), Dai Hughes, The Duke of Westminster

Blue Peter had launched a charity campaign at the same time and admitted that they had virtually no response from Wrexham because the whole town was preoccupied with its own Operation Christmas Child.

LEGO GAVE £2,000 PLUS SIX PALLETS OF LEGO (WEIGHING TWO TONS!) AND 2,000 BABY RATTLES. **KELLOGG'S** DONATED BREAKFAST CEREALS. **JOHNSON & JOHNSON** PROVIDED AN ARTICULATED LORRY FULL OF MEDICAL EQUIPMENT. **LANDSCAPE DEVELOPMENTS** DONATED 300 BOTTLES OF FRESH WATER. GLAXO PHARMACEUTICALS, LONDON, GAVE £30,000-WORTH OF ANTIBIOTICS. **VODAFONE** SUPPLIED A PHONE FOR THE TRIP AND PAID FOR THE USE OF IT. MAELOR HOSPITAL GENEROUSLY SUPPLIED MATTRESSES, BLANKETS, HOSPITAL TROLLEYS, BOWLS, BEDPANS, URINALS, CRUTCHES, WALKING AIDS AND LAMPS. THE CROWN INN, LLAY, ORGANISED A SPONSORED BEEF BURGER EATING COMPETITION. **RUBERY OWEN ROCKWELL** PROVIDED A 40-FOOT ARTICULATED LORRY CRAMMED WITH SUPPLIES, PLUS TWO DRIVERS. **ARLINGTON TRUCK CENTRE** OFFERED TO FILL UP THE TRUCK WITH FUEL. **R AND R NAYLORS**, WELSHPOOL, SUPPLIED 300 CARDBOARD BOXES. JCB WROTE A CHEQUE FOR £1,000. **HAWARDEN MOTORS** DONATED 10% OF EVERY HIRE DEAL THEY ARRANGED IN THE RUN UP TO CHRISTMAS.

MILUPA GAVE £4,000 - WORTH OF DEHYDRATED BABY FOOD. **HOGANS** CLOTHES SHOP IN WREXHAM GAVE SIX BOXES OF BRAND NEW CLOTHES FOR THE CHILDREN. **LINDLEY PLANT** PROVIDED 50 GALLONS OF DIESEL. **VAUXHALL MOTORS** HELPED WITH PACKAGING THE AID. **HALFORDS** MET ALL THE LIGHTING NEEDS FOR THE LORRIES. **SCOTT'S NIGHTCLUB** GAVE ALL THEIR TAKINGS FROM A SPECIAL NIGHT IN DECEMBER. **WREXHAM WIRE** DONATED 20 MATTRESSES. **DEEP PAN PIZZA** WAITRESSING STAFF IN CHESTER DONATED THEIR TIPS, WORTH AROUND £500. **BURTONS BISCUITS**, WARRINGTON, GAVE SEVERAL PALLETS OF BISCUITS. **LEVER INDUSTRIES**, RUNCORN, DONATED TEN TONS OF TOILETRIES AND CLEANING MATERIALS. **BNFL** AT CAPENHURST GAVE £1,000 AND THERMAL SUITS FOR THE DRIVERS, AND ARRANGED FOR THEIR SISTER COMPANY IN GERMANY TO ORGANISE A NIGHT'S STAY IN A HOTEL FOR THE DRIVERS. **DELMAR TRAVEL** PAID FOR THE DRIVERS' INSURANCE. **WREXHAM LORD MAYOR**, COUNCILLOR MALCOLM WILLIAMS GAVE £500 - AND A WHIP ROUND BY HIS STAFF DOUBLED IT. AND HUNDREDS OF OTHERS GAVE WHAT THEY COULD.

Phil Roberts, Presenter, Marcher Sound

Fundraising for the first trip was essentially spearheaded by Marcher Sound. In the week before Operation Christmas Child's departure a new target figure of £50,000 was calculated. On Friday 7 December, five days before the convoy left, the total stood at £42,000. Marcher pulled out all the stops, with presenter Phil Roberts live on air pleading with listeners, 'Come on everybody. We can do it - do it - do it!' All Marcher DJs sent out the same message, 'What a lot of lovely people you are out there! Give, give, and give till it hurts!'

The phones went wild, people burst through the doors carrying buckets of cash and handfuls of cheques. By 6 p.m. over £8,000 was pledged. With the help of Marcher, Operation Christmas Child had burst through the £50,000 barrier in one day. By the Monday another £10,000 was in the kitty - 'giving fever' was rampant!

On Thursday 13 December 1990 Wrexham did itself proud as it turned out in full force to give its mission of mercy to Romania a moving send off. While the team tucked into a full cooked breakfast with the Lord Mayor, over 5,000 people gathered outside the Guildhall.

Despite the bitterly-cold December weather, flags were waving, and everyone was cheering and singing along to the music provided by Marcher Sound. Live bands, DJs, and a massive carnival were all part of the event. Emotions were highly charged and people were crying everywhere. These men were going into the unknown, and no one was quite sure what they would find.

'At the start of the campaign we hoped to take two small trucks to Romania and raise about £15,000 in cash, but the response from the people of Wrexham and the North West took everyone by surprise. By the time of leaving, more than £500,000 in aid and £60,000 in cash had been raised. We were overwhelmed by it all, and were so grateful to everyone involved for all their hard work.'

Dave Cooke

'The atmosphere was electric. It had been the town's project - everyone from the big businesses to grannies had given what they could.'

Dave Cooke

Paul Wilcox prepares to leave for Romania

'We needed the unforgettable send off from home and small pieces of encouragement because three days on the road in a 7.5 ton lorry was not the best trip in the world. The buzz of the send off carried us right through Germany. We couldn't have asked for better support from the people back home - it was fantastic.'

Dave Cooke

Not everything went smoothly. As the trucks arrived to be loaded up a day or so earlier, an engine gasket blew. No replacement could be found so two heroes, Richard Pugh and Derek Collis, stepped in and sweated into the early hours of the morning to rebuild a 'new' engine free of charge. The truck was ready just in the nick of time!

Dave Cooke's original idea had been to take a couple of trucks over to Eastern Europe. Eventually seven lorries, decorated with tinsel, balloons and messages from the children of Wrexham, revved up their engines and slowly moved through the crowds. Looking out on the sea of faces through their tear-filled eyes, the team of 18 drivers and a film crew could hardly have had a more rousing send off.

On each street corner crowds were queuing to wave them off. No one wanted to miss out on the mission that had brought the whole community together. 'All the drivers agreed that the atmosphere at the send off was amazing,' recalled journalist Paul Wilcox. 'To see all those young people crying, it was almost as though they were experiencing some of the things we were going to experience when we got to Romania.'

The convoy headed south from Wrexham receiving an incredible reception everywhere it went. Operators at the Dartford Tunnel waved them through the tollgates without charging, P&O Ferries supplied a free meal on the ferry across the Channel, and throughout Germany they were given free fuel because they were taking aid to Romania. On the streets they often caused a stir as people stopped and stared at them, and other lorry drivers frequently acknowledged the convoy with the blast of a horn and a friendly wave.

Convoy drivers get ready to hit the road

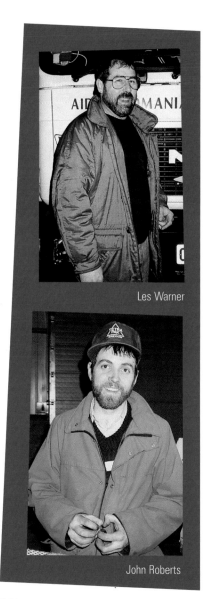

Les Warner

John Roberts

Early morning in Cologne, Germany, the convoy left the autobahn to be treated to breakfast and a warm reception by Uranit, a German company that had connections with one of the drivers. Later a director of Uranit wrote to Operation Christmas Child to tell them of his company's reaction to their visit:

> I would like to thank you and your comrades for the marvellous atmosphere you brought to us on this cold dark morning.
> A colleague of mine has described to me the same feelings I had when he said, 'These people from Wrexham were surrounded by a strange atmosphere of joy and happiness, although they were so tired having driven through the night.'

As they moved south through the mountain passes of Austria and down into Hungary, the adrenalin began to wear off. The bitter winter cold was digging in. Temperatures dropped to sub-zero through the night in the trucks and someone always had to stay awake to keep watch for gypsies. But the experience proved to be a steep learning curve. The 7.5-ton lorries were less than ideal and wouldn't be used again, and with each border the crew gained savvy in dealing with the guards, learning to negotiate without bribery.

Once in Hungary they were quick to realise the country was in quite a mess and the police had very little control, so the convoy became a law unto themselves! With no motorway systems and hundreds of small junctions, a familiar call on the radios became, 'Box it up.' Each truck had its own radio and when the leader approached traffic lights, the driver would advise them to 'box it up' by closing within a foot of each other, nose to tail, and driving straight through. And so the convoy slowly moved through Hungary, humorous radio calls building up their morale as they began the descent into Romania.

Throughout the whole journey the team had feared an accident would cast a dark shadow over the trip. As darkness fell on the Saturday their nightmare became reality. Just after entering the capital, Budapest, the ROR juggernaut leading the way screeched to a halt. Driver John Kight broke the news that the convoy was stuck because the bridge ahead was too low to negotiate. Two dreadful hours followed. The co-drivers leapt down from their cabs carrying torches to help the trucks back up along the three miles of winding roads in the pitch dark.

Almost at once a car skidded round a corner on ice and crashed into a stationary van. The potential for a very nasty accident was increasing by the minute. Surprisingly, help came in the form of a shabby Trabant car with flashing roof lights. The clapped-out vehicle pulled up and a smiley chap called Rudi climbed out to offer his assistance. 'He appeared out of nowhere and was like an angel,' Dave recalled. Rudi proceeded to use his vehicle like a New York squad car, forcing the oncoming traffic that was flying round the corner at them into taking some notice of the danger ahead. Rudi helped them to turn the trucks round in the road to save them reversing, and led them through the town and to a little place in Budapest where they could stay for the night.

Next morning they enlisted the help of 'the best taxi driver in town' to guide them out of the city, avoiding low bridges and any other potentially-hazardous obstacles.

ROR Juggernaut

Rudi

Clive Coleclough

Dave Cooke

Right from the start they grasped the need for a healthy team spirit. At the heart of this was a focus on the Christian faith that was so central to the lives of the four men who formed the initial team. Before hitting the road each morning they would begin with a briefing followed by a short talk and prayer led by Clive Coleclough. Clive is a Justice of the Peace from Wrexham who was the unofficial 'spiritual adviser' on the trip (and is now a member of the Samaritan's Purse UK board). 'We were a bunch of very different characters,' explained Dave. 'We were from all sorts of walks of life, and soon realised everyone had different needs. It was all new to us, but we had to learn fast how to manage a team of amazingly-different people who'd never met until a few weeks before.' A sense of humour was essential for relieving tension and keeping them going when everyone felt completely exhausted.

Dave and Dai headed up the team, and, with hindsight, are the first to admit that not all the decisions they made were the best. However, it was a new role for them, and they were learning as they went along. 'By the time we arrived in Romania, we'd learnt that you fuel all the trucks at the same time, keep them together, and make sure everyone tows the line. It took a lot of fun, and a lot of frustration to make these discoveries,' Dave admitted.

Problems hit as they arrived at the Hungarian-Romania border. Hungarian border guards were particularly awkward, apparently angered that the aid was going to Romania when their own country had desperate needs too. 'Why you no bring us aid?' grunted one guard. Their resentment was understandable. Romania was under the media spotlight but Hungary, too, was poor and bleak. There was no evidence of Christmas celebrations for the Hungarians and yet everyone was heading to Romania.

Even the dirty tinsel tied to the trucks fascinated the border guards. Some wanted to keep it for themselves - a sad indication of how cut off they had been.

Lengthy deliberations ensued, resulting in Operation Christmas Child offering the guards 'gifts' of paracetamol tablets, biscuits and chocolate. The convoy eventually crossed the Romanian border on the morning of Monday 17 December. In Dave's words, it was 'like driving through a quarry at night, with loads of pot-holes and no street lights'. Traffic was minimal, except for horse-drawn carts jingling along unlit streets without warning lights. At petrol stations cars were queuing to wait for fuel, sometimes as far as three miles. The guide informed Dave, 'Here, people waiting all weekend for petrol.'

As soon as the sun came up they were hit with shock at this new culture. Reporter Paul Wilcox likened it to 'a scene straight out of George Orwell's 1984'. The shops were stripped bare, apart from champagne and empty pickle jars. The place smelled terrible and they suddenly felt desperately insecure. 'We realised we were on our own and it felt terrible,' Dave admitted. 'I don't know how people coped in these areas without God to trust in.'

'I sensed a real oppression here among the people. They don't have any expression on their faces. Something inside seems to have died.'
Beverley Turner, 21,
student at St Helen's College, who filmed the trip.

'Wrexham, home and friends were a world away as we drove our convoy into a land that is both medieval and primitive.'

Paul Wilcox,
Wrexham Mail Reporter

Oradea, Romania

Dai Hughes & Dave Cooke

A meeting that evening at the Second Baptist Church in Oradea opened their eyes to the spiritual hunger that pervaded the country. Operation Christmas Child volunteers began handing out small gifts and food to the crowds that surrounded them, but outside the church a hand slipped through the window of the chase car that led the convoy. A shy voice whispered fearfully, 'Please, have you just one Bible?' They had lived through a spiritual famine during the Communist reign of the past 50 years, and this was a cry from the heart.

That night Dave had a secret rendezvous with his contacts. The Romanians were piling on pressure to take control of the supplies themselves, but Dave was adamant. Operation Christmas Child had agreed to deliver the aid personally, not least to ensure that it didn't find its way onto the black market.

Nothing could have prepared the Operation Christmas Child team for the horror that awaited them when they arrived at the first orphanage. Driving through impoverished peasant farms and villages, the landscape threw them back a couple of generations. The gates of the orphanage were obstructed by a crowd of gypsies, desperate to get their hands on the supplies so they could sell them on. Determined to reach the children, the volunteers climbed out of the trucks, filled their arms with shoe boxes and pushed their way into the muddy grey courtyard. As they looked up, they saw a huddle of gaunt-faced children staring blankly at them through a barred window ahead.

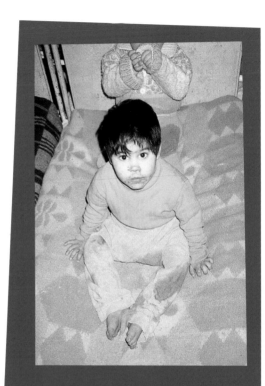

'Seeing it on television is one thing, but actually being in the room, with kids that looked like battery chickens all around you, three or four to a cot, with their wrists and ankles tied up, just rocking, was so distressing.'
Dave Cooke

A deathly quiet hung over the first room they entered, disturbed only by the clicking noise of the children grinding their own teeth out of boredom. Urine-soaked cots and the solitary lavatory for more than a hundred children released an unbearable stench throughout the building. Each door that was opened revealed another room full of children starved of love and affection. They looked like little moon people: they had never seen a toy in their lives and just sat staring into space. One member of the convoy remarked, 'It was amazing that they were even alive.'

The tough truck drivers were reduced to tears and many were forced to leave the room, overwhelmed by an atrocity they could never have imagined. They would go outside and build each other up before going back in again, but all felt emotionally wrecked.

'Each room seemed to reveal some new obscenity. I felt myself slip into a state of shock and spent the rest of the day in a limbo state, suspended between dream and nightmare.'
Paul Wilcox, Reporter, Wrexham Mail

In an attempt to build up a massive land army, Nicolae Ceausescu had insisted that every woman have at least four babies. But the regime he had subjected them to meant that the women couldn't afford to support the children and so the orphanage system came into effect. Thousands of little lives were institutionalised in these houses of horror while the 'best' were weeded out and directed into prostitution by the Securitate.

According to World Vision, working in Romania at the time, without receiving aid up to 50 per cent of the children in the orphanages would die.

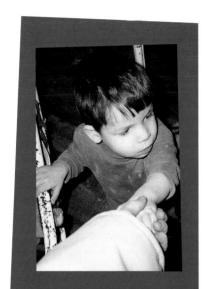

'We would give sweets to the children and they wouldn't know what they were. We'd have to say, "Take the wrapper off and eat it," but they'd put the whole thing in their mouth, not realising they couldn't eat the paper. They'd had nothing and it was mind-blowing for us.'

Dave Cooke

'One young boy stands out in my mind. He didn't know what to do with the shoe box when we gave it to him. As we took things out he kissed each item. So overwhelmed was he by the gift that his legs gave way and he just fainted.'

Dave Cooke

On the day Operation Christmas Child visited that orphanage, a small flicker of light shone into the dark lives of these horribly-neglected children. The moment the children began receiving their parcels was wonderful. The atmosphere in the room burst into life. Drab, emotionless and vacant faces were transformed with smiles and laughter. Some were too overwhelmed to react, but others ran to embrace, kiss, and cuddle the volunteers. A rocking horse was placed in the middle of one room and the children touched and smiled and stroked the wooden horse. Some didn't know what it meant to play, and sitting on the horse was the first experience of what it felt like to enjoy life.

Moments of sad comedy invaded the excitement. Some little children were intrigued by sweet smelling packages and were found chewing on bars of soap. Others were happily sucking on tubes of toothpaste.

The staff that looked after the children were paid a few pence per week, and had very few resources, but despite this they wanted to feed the drivers. It was food that back home the drivers wouldn't have even given to pigs, but the willingness of the Romanians to give what they had amazed the team and they made an effort to return the generosity with gratitude. The smell was awful and the plates dirty, but as one of the team said, 'We've given thanks for this food, we'd better sit and eat it.'

As they got back into the trucks they began to build each other up for the next job. It was a soul-destroying mission and they were all struggling. Some were filled with anger at the corruption and injustice. Why have the rich got all the money? Why are these kids suffering? Why is the government not doing anything? Look at Ceausescu's palace - what's gone wrong?

As they left the orphanage, gypsies thronged round the trucks, hoping to get something for themselves. A nuisance, even a danger, to the convoy, the drivers revved up the engines to bypass them quickly. But then it struck them. They were poor too. They weren't terrible people. Just like the kids in the orphanage, they desperately needed to be loved and to share in Christmas.

Dave's four-year-old daughter, Sarah, had put a tatty doll in her daddy's bag as he left. As they handed out gifts to the gypsies, a little girl caught Dave's eye. Her face was grubby and her clothes in tatters, but something in him thought this was just the kind of girl Sarah would like to give her doll to.

'When we returned to "The Halfway House" orphanage at Easter the bedroom walls were covered with the wrapping paper from the shoe boxes they had received at Christmas.'

Les Lever, journalist

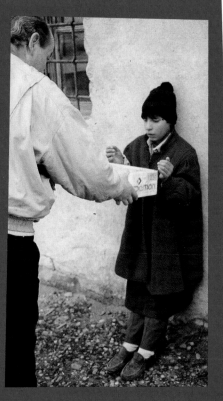

'The Halfway House' was the name given by Operation Christmas Child to an orphanage they visited on a number of occasions. German aid workers were already doing a lot of work there so they just took in goodies for the kids. Dave recalled one particularly moving incident from this place: 'Each of the kids had just been given a shoe box. We piled back in the trucks and the convoy started to move off when I saw her in the side mirror. She was a young girl, standing in a corner, just rocking backwards and forwards in the cold. I radioed to see if we had another shoe box. Someone found one and took it across to her. When she opened it, there was a beautiful doll inside. It was as if this box was for this girl. Out of all those thousands of boxes we carried, this box was meant for this little girl.'

Liviu Balas

A group of young conscripts were enlisted to unload the trucks. Eager for Western currency to help feed their young families, the soldiers offered their belts and guns in exchange. As they passed the aid along the line, their jackets would begin to bulge. Dave said: 'We realised it was unfair to ask these guys to handle Western goods when they had hungry children at home too.' Instead, they allowed the soldiers to help themselves.

A prime concern for Dave was to ensure that the aid made it to those who needed it most. In the weeks of preparation they had made contact with Christians in Romania and arranged meetings with people they could trust.

A spectacular journey over the Caucasus mountain range led them down into the city of Cluj. Their instructions were to meet a man who would be standing beside a road sign on the outskirts of the town at a certain time. He was Liviu Balas, a contact given to Dave by Gary Cox, who runs the Bristol-based aid charity Eurovangelism. It was Liviu, complete with his huge beard, who would meet them each day on the side of the road at a pre-arranged location to give them directions to the next place of need. He'd given his life to working for these desperate Romanian kids and set up an organisation called Ecce Homo, Latin for 'Behold the Man'. Dave said, 'He is one of the most amazing guys I ever met working in that country. He was able to set us in just the right direction.'

Cluj Hospital was a crumbling building where dingy corridors led to decaying wards. The building itself needed demolition, but the horror stories that were waiting inside were even more disturbing. One doctor told how a week earlier he had performed a Caesarean section without anaesthetic. Worse still, the scalpels were so old and blunt that a stabbing action had to be used to make an incision.

The men rolled up their sleeves and helped in any way they could, from unloading medical supplies and delivering them to different departments, to helping set up a new cardiac unit. Countless lives were saved through that one delivery alone.

Phil Hughes with a child in Cluj orphanage

Adrian Jarvis with Romanian child

'I had a packet of McVitie's biscuits in my pocket. I took one out, walked up to one of the cleaning staff in the hospital, and gave it to her. The next few moments were mind-blowing. She broke the biscuit into six pieces and gave them to her staff. It was just one McVitie's biscuit. I gave her the whole packet and she broke down in tears.'

Dave Cooke

Imagine being in a hospital where doctors toss a coin to decide whether you or the person in the next bed will receive the last course of antibiotics. Dave saw this scene being played out in reality. An operation was taking place and the Operation Christmas Child team, in their grubby clothes, were invited into the operating theatre. Hardly any oxygen was left to keep the patient breathing. The surgeon told Dave, 'Septicaemia has set in on this patient and one next door. We don't know which one to give the antibiotics to so we're going to toss a coin to decide.' How wonderful that Dave was able to tell them not to worry - he had enough antibiotics in the trucks for 50 patients. With that he was able to hand over the drugs, and both lives were saved.

As they left Romania, plans to return were already starting to form in Dave's mind. There was much to think about, many dreams for the future, so much to do. As the convoy neared Wrexham, they turned the radio on to hear the familiar strains of Marcher Sound. Chris Rea's 'Driving home for Christmas' was played especially for them and it's a tune that will always provoke special memories for that very first team.

Just before entering their hometown, the trucks stopped. Everyone grouped together and said their goodbyes. They'd experienced something together that would make its own mark on each of their lives. Emotions were highly charged. Tough guys who had been thrown together at the beginning, with all their differences and foibles, now shared a very deep bond. There was something there that they didn't want to lose. Their goodbyes over, they were ready to make their way to the warehouse to receive a hero's welcome and be reunited with family and friends.

They returned to Wrexham just a couple of days before Christmas and the contrast with Romania could not have been starker. Dave remembers being irritated at a local supermarket: 'People were squabbling about what they were going to get, like what size of turkey. I felt like shouting - "Look, people in Romania have nothing. Stop arguing."' Each one of them found it a struggle to cope with the emotional pressure as they gave and received presents on Christmas Day. Dave admitted, 'After what we'd experienced my mind kept going back, and blank.' It took him a while to adjust, but says it is something he's better able to cope with now: 'I don't think it gets any easier, though. The day I get blasé about it, I'll pack it all in.'

Over a decade later, Dave still retains a deep level of personal involvement in the work, and his compassion for suffering children is as strong as ever. The work of Operation Christmas Child has gone from strength to strength, bringing love and happiness to millions of children. Much has happened since those early days in Wrexham, and Operation Christmas Child is now part of the international charity Samaritan's Purse. It delivers aid - and the message of hope that is found in Jesus Christ - to victims of poverty, natural disaster and war around the world.

But what drove Dave to give what he had to those who have nothing? Was he always heading towards the role of 'Father Christmas' to tens of thousands of children? His former headmaster obviously didn't think so! Dave recalls being told, 'Cooke, you'll never achieve anything!' before being promptly told to leave the premises for good. It's amazing what God can do with a person when He gets hold of a life and chooses to use it for good.

Dave Cooke

'You'll never achieve anything'

An unusual start

Not only is Dave Cooke the father of four, he was also one of four children. His life began in a little terraced house in Chester. Quite literally too - he was born in the front room! He and elder brother Paul were followed by two younger sisters, Jan and Rachel.

While both Dave's parents were Christians, for most of his childhood they were part of the Exclusive Brethren, a group who believed in drastically restricting their contact with the outside world. This made for an unusual childhood in many senses, and had a profound effect on Dave's early years. The hard line approach to discipline, the struggle to be accepted in the face of isolation, and his early realisation of the fragility of life all seemed incongruous with the loving person of Jesus Christ he had learnt about.

Although some of Dave's heroes and role models based their entire lives on their relationship with God, Dave just couldn't see how this Being or Person fitted into the world around him. It was several years before he realised he might be approaching faith the wrong way. Instead of trying to fit God into his world, in fact it was him - ordinary Dave Cooke - who needed to be slotted into God's vast plans. But first he had to let go of the controls. It was a tough journey, but one that began on a little street called Derby Place, Chester...

'I can remember quite a happy childhood, apart from the awful restrictions. It wasn't all gloom, there were happy moments.'

Dave Cooke

Two brothers lived up the road, Paul and John. They were the same age as Dave and his brother Paul, and together they made up a gang of firm friends: 'We each had bikes and we went everywhere and did everything together during school hours.'

Dave's Mum stood for no nonsense with the boys. Although Dave and Paul were close friends, like all brothers, they had their moments. As they were restricted in how much they could play with other children their Dad used to buy Airfix models for them. One of the biggest models they made was the battleship HMS Hood. It was about two feet long and had taken hours of gluing and painting before it was finished. Dave and Paul began arguing over who had done the most work on it, and who it really belonged to. As they bickered over the precious work, their Mum picked it up and snapped it over her knee and gave them half each! As Dave admitted: 'That gives you a good picture of her no-mucking-about, no-questions-asked, black and white approach. There was no way we were going to argue over a possession again!'

Dave and Paul Cooke

'We were fortunate to have a vehicle even throughout our childhood. It was a van that had meat in it throughout the week. We used to wash it on Saturday morning, and then put cardboard down and sit on the wheel hubs in the back. I can still remember the smell from the drying blood - it was awful! But we had a vehicle and were the only family in our row of houses who did.'

Dave Cooke

An incredible woman lived next door to the Cookes. Mrs Valelly, known to Dave affectionately as 'Auntie Betty', had eight children of her own, but treated Dave as an extra son. 'Because we weren't allowed a television in our house we used to sneak across there when Mum and Dad went out, and she used to let us in through the back door to go in and watch television with all her kids,' Dave remembers. She loved Dave and his siblings - and still does. Aunt Betty lives in the same house on Derby Place - exactly the same as it was forty years ago - and the Cookes continue to visit this lady who had such an influence on them as they grew up.

Dave was quite a handful as a child. He'd often be locked in his bedroom for misbehaving, but would open the window, climb down the drainpipe and run away. His unruly behaviour was possibly a kickback from the rigid regime he was raised in, where there was no real outlet for his energy. Whatever the cause, however, everyone around him found him very difficult to control.

On one occasion the four boys were cycling home from school and discovered a short cut on the mile-and-a-half journey. The route took them over a humpback bridge and, as they approached it, a bus came up behind them. The boys cycled into the middle of the road and started doing wheelies, standing on the seats and cycling with no hands. It was all intended to be good fun and once over the bridge they cycled off down a side road while the bus carried on.

The bus driver was unimpressed. He went round the block, stopped at the end of the road where the boys were hiding and gave them each a dressing down and a clip round the ear!

They arrived home for tea at five o'clock and as their Mum put the meal on the table she turned and said, 'There were some stupid boys today fooling around in front of the bus I was on. I hope you two never do that kind of thing.' Dave and Paul just looked at each other and weren't quite sure how to respond. It wasn't until a few years later that they told her the truth.

Paul, Dave and Jan Cooke

'I must have been hard to deal with as a kid; I had so many clips around the ear. That kind of thing isn't allowed anymore, but I needed that discipline.'

Dave Cooke

Exclusive Brethren

The Exclusive Brethren had a controlling impact on many aspects of their family life, asserting influence on the way they were educated, the friendships they had and the activities in which they were involved. Even the way they organised their finances, the type of employment they undertook or how they ran a business came under question. But while there were many negative aspects, they did enjoy very close friendships and its teaching instilled an early awareness of God in Dave, even if this was marred by some of its extremes.

From an early age Dave was conscious of God and knew Jesus was much more than a Galilean carpenter who had been crucified two thousand years earlier. A delightful man called Andrew Abernethy had explained this to Dave when he was just a little lad. He'd told him, 'You know, David, Jesus died especially for you. God sent His Son to die for you.' It had a big impact on Dave, and from the age of eight or nine he would go with Andrew as he preached in different towns, keen to hear him speak about Jesus. It was a personal tragedy for Dave when his first 'hero', Andrew, was killed in a road accident some time later.

With no television at home, Dave wasn't like his contemporaries, who had heroes like George Best. Instead he looked up to people within the Exclusive Brethren - 'real men' whom he admired. Sadly, the life of another role model was to be cut short. Michael Lloyd was knocked off his bike on his way home one evening. He was just twenty-two. It was as Dave peered into the open coffin in the Lloyd family home, and saw a dead body for the first time, that he began to ask questions: 'Why did Michael have to die? What is life for? Isn't it a waste if we end up lying there dead and that's the end.'

This apparent waste conflicted with the God that Andrew and Michael had described to him. Dave admitted: 'I was aware of the creation around me. The countryside is fascinating - it's always given me a sense of awe. There is a verse in the Bible that says the cattle on a thousand hills are God's. I knew this, but I couldn't work out the sadness and the questions.'

'Dave has always been a very caring, loving person. Even as a boy, he was good with smaller children and really looked after them. But mixed in with this he was also full of fun and mischief. It was never that quiet when Dave was around!'

Dave's Mum

School

Being brought up within the strict, rigid regime of the Exclusive Brethren made for a rather lonely and unusual childhood. Opportunities to make friends at school were cut short as Dave was forced to eat alone and excluded from after-school sports activities. This tight-knit religious community felt they should only mix in their own circles. The children were even barred from joining in morning assemblies and Religious Education classes for fear that the Exclusive Brethren teaching would be undermined.

'As someone who loved sport, being barred from taking part was a major blow to me. I believe my background affected my schooling, because it singled me out - I wasn't part of the team. This was right from a very young age, when I started school. Christmas parties came round and the teachers would make a great fuss over me because they wanted me to be a part of it. So they'd go to great lengths to sit me at a table on my own. It was terrible. I just felt awful.'

Dave Cooke

A strong and determined child, Dave became the class clown in an attempt to win the affection of his peers. Despite being singled out and excluded from any team or year-group activities, Dave was often the class ringleader. 'If there was ever any fun, trouble or jokes being played you could be sure I'd be there in the forefront of things,' Dave recalled.

'I had an odd schooling experience, but I wasn't bullied by the other kids. Because I was one of the harder or stronger guys in the class I could handle myself well. I was the clown of the class, which was an attention-seeking ploy.'

Dave Cooke

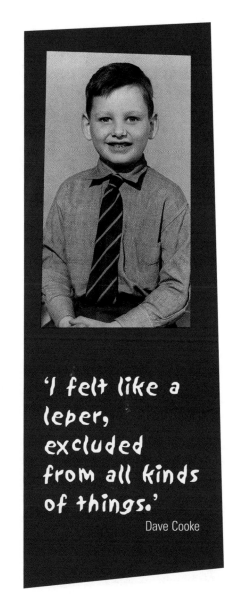

'I felt like a leper, excluded from all kinds of things.'

Dave Cooke

47

'As a kid I didn't rub shoulders with those who came from the nicer part of town. It was always the lower or the poorer person that I gravitated towards, the ones who had been to borstal and come back. I suppose it is the same now. I'd rather spend time with those type of people than with the hoity-toities or the Hooray Henrys.'

Dave Cooke

Leadership skills came naturally and in the playground he'd be the one to get things organised, to set up teams and initiate ideas. Perhaps it was during this period, when he was forced to develop a certain level of resistance, that he learned the merit in not accepting things the way they are.

'I was an initiator even at school, and I enjoyed that position. I suppose in many ways, it went along with being liked.'

Dave Cooke

While Dave often found himself at the centre of trouble at school, he wasn't one to hold grudges: 'I often used to fall out with somebody one day, and we'd fight and tear each other to pieces. But you could bet your bottom dollar that within twenty-four hours I'd be his best friend.' Dave had a sense of compassion even as a youngster struggling with his rebellion. He'd often find himself feeling sorry for someone he'd just beaten up, and he also looked out for the neglected person in the class.

At fourteen, Dave was glad to see the back of school - and the feeling was mutual. Mr Fox, the headmaster, told him: 'Cooke, you'll never achieve anything. You're a waster.'

Academic studies weren't exactly Dave's forté, but he had done well in the practical subjects, and enjoyed them too. Admittedly these classes did give him freedom to fool around as well, whether it was throwing things around the workshop, gluing coats to the wall or nailing books to the desk. Two teachers did relate to Dave and encouraged him to persevere. 'Sid Old taught me woodwork and maths, and I just remember that he related to me and at the same time didn't let me get away with much. Then there was Alan Mort. He was a sportsman - a cricketer - and taught gardening. He was my form teacher and encouraged me a lot. Again, he was a disciplinarian, but he was real, and you could have a laugh with him too.'

On the wrong side of the law

A regular paper round offered Dave independence, especially when he left school. Getting up at 6 a.m. and then doing the same round again at night was a good discipline and paid two shillings and six pence a week. Very soon though, he and his friends began stealing from the shop they were working for. What began as petty theft quickly escalated to hundreds of cigarettes that they would sell on. 'Initially it was because we needed more money, and we also enjoyed the "business" aspect of it. It also was the buzz of the unknown. And that was the start; I soon found myself getting in with a bad crowd.'

Fortunately for Dave, he and his friends were caught one day, and it gave him a sufficient shock to stop him falling further down that route. Stealing bikes to make other bikes had been another of their 'hobbies'. The police caught up with them and knocked on the door of his house. Dave's Dad answered and was devastated that his son had been involved in this activity and brought the family name into disrepute. His father's reaction once the detectives had left was quite remarkable. Each day he prayed with the family, and on this occasion he prayed that good would come out of this situation and the mess would be sorted out. 'Up until that time I looked at praying about that kind of thing as wrong. Why should I be praying? It was me that had fouled up, so I had no right to ask to get out of the mess,' Dave remembers. Another side of him was desperate for it to stay out of the papers and for it to be sorted out without his Mum and Dad experiencing further humiliation: 'The real punishment was what I went through. I couldn't hack the thought of what it would do to Mum and Dad. I was really struggling with life and the mess I was in.' The police came back and said they had enough evidence to take Dave to court, but that they would let it pass as a warning.

'I soon found myself getting in with a bad crowd.'

Dave Cooke

Tragedy

After leaving school Dave became an apprentice joiner, and signed up for a college course that would provide some qualifications to take him through life. It was a new scene and he found he had to grow up very quickly, being disciplined with his studies. This time he was there by choice; no one was going to make him work.

Dave had found a good friend in Ian Atkinson - 'Akers' as he was known to the boys. He was an only son, who had a great sense of humour and went to college on day-release from his job with the local council. A gang from college used to enjoy poaching in their spare time, and it was while they were out in the fields one afternoon that tragedy hit.

Three or four of them, including Dave's friend Akers, were crouching behind hedges, enjoying the sport. One of the boys fired a shot, and it hit Akers right through the head. The incident had a profound effect on the entire class, but especially the boys who had witnessed it. Murder charges were initially talked about, but it was eventually ruled as accidental death. The funeral raised the same issues over the waste of life that Dave had struggled with when his two mentors had been killed.

Leaving the Exclusive Brethren

The hard questions that Dave couldn't answer, and the confined lifestyle of the Exclusive Brethren, led him to tell his parents, 'I can't cope with this Brethren thing anymore.' His brother Paul joined the protest. At the next meeting, their father informed the Brethren that the boys would not be returning. The Cookes were advised to throw the boys out of their home. Because the Cookes refused to do this they were 'withdrawn' from the Exclusive Brethren. This took them into a complete unknown. All their lives they had been separated from the world around them, their whole life being bound up with the denomination. In spite of this, they knew things were not right, and the Cookes stuck with there decision to leave.

A fresh start

For Dave, the immediate effect was that he signed up to the college football team, enjoying for the first time the freedom to participate in sporting activities. As a family they joined a local church - the Chester City Mission. It was a place where the Bible was taught without extreme emphases or legalistic views, but where they learned more about the Christ who could forgive their sins and who loved them unconditionally.

The pastor was an ex-Welsh guard called David Coombes. This amazing character, well over six feet tall, was able to get alongside Dave and understand where he was at. He wasn't afraid to be blunt, and tell Dave to get his act together. The pastor's army background instilled respect in Dave, but the sincerity of his faith and his genuine care for Dave made an even greater impression.

'He called a spade a spade, and that was just what I needed. Many a time I was taken into his office and put back on the straight and narrow.'
Dave Cooke on David Coombes of the Chester City Mission

Dave became involved in the Chester Youth Council, and helped set up a youth club in his local area. It was within this Christian group, Contact, that Dave really found his home. As goalkeeper of their football team, Dave enjoyed playing in local matches. Weekend trips away with the group often involved him taking services for churches around North Wales and North West England.

Eric Greene, who ran Contact, was a great inspiration to Dave: 'What amazed me about Eric was his loyalty to the kids in his care. He was the most dedicated guy working with kids I've ever come across.'

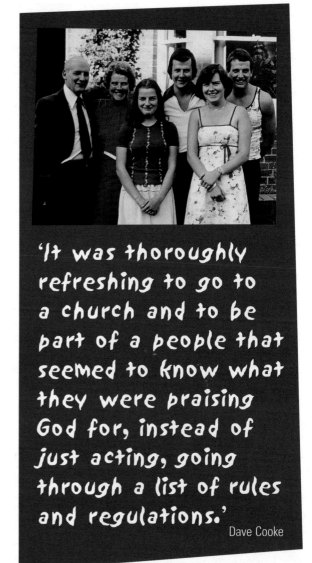

'It was thoroughly refreshing to go to a church and to be part of a people that seemed to know what they were praising God for, instead of just acting, going through a list of rules and regulations.'
Dave Cooke

Dave's involvement in youth work sparked off an interest in childcare, particularly work with under-privileged kids. It was the mid-seventies and the era of strikes had begun. It hit the building trade in a big way, and Dave found himself out of work. He had no inclination to picket, and so he looked in a different direction. It was his first step towards reaching out to children.

A friend of the family, Des Frost, recognised Dave's love and dedication towards young people. Although he was aware that Dave was not officially qualified in the field, he found Dave his first job as a Childcare Officer, an area he worked in for five years. This stood him in good stead for the work he would be involved in as Operation Christmas Child developed a few years later.

Romance

Dave could hardly have found love in someone more different than his wife-to-be, Gill. They first met at a Christian concert in Chester Town Hall and Dave found himself instantly captivated by this girl with an incredible smile and amazingly gentle attitude. She was well educated, and her respectable Christian parents weren't immediately taken with the character of dubious reputation with whom their daughter was spending time. Neither was Gill! It took some persuading on Dave's part to win her over. They went out for a few years until Gill left to study Pharmacy at Manchester University and broke off the relationship. The tough Dave Cooke found himself broken-hearted and threw himself into his work, outdoor pursuits, and activities with young people.

But it was his interest in motorbiking that eventually brought the couple back together. He and a friend took off to go round Wales one summer, touring the countryside on their bikes. When they stopped off at the seaside town of Newquay, Dave met up with Gill, who was working with United Beach Missions, running a kind of Sunday School on the beach with daily activities for holidaymakers. Dave couldn't resist the opportunity to tell Gill that his feelings for her had remained as strong, and they started seeing each other again. A few months down the line Gill became Mrs Dave Cooke.

Dave and Gill

Business Disasters

Working in childcare put a great deal of strain on Dave and he started thinking about returning 'to the tools'. He had managed to keep up joinery in his spare time, so when the opportunity presented itself he decided it was time to return to the carpenter's bench. He enjoyed being back doing this kind of practical work, but still had a hankering for more. It wasn't what he wanted to be doing when he was forty and he was looking for a more management-orientated role. So he embarked on a business venture, fitting kitchens. Unfortunately, the business partnership ran into problems, with the result that Dave and Gill, who by now had two young children, lost their house to the bank. They were left with nothing. While they battled with this financial strain, they also had to deal with a personal sadness. Gill was pregnant at the time, but they lost the child. All Dave had worked and hoped for seemed to be disintegrating around him. Yet his faith in the 'God who doesn't make mistakes' and the partnership of his incredibly-supportive wife kept him going.

'I remember living in digs one Christmas with a couple of my nippers and thinking, "What on earth am I doing here?" Everything around me seemed to be falling apart. But you know God is there and He's got His eye on you. You've just got to hang on and pray that God will look after you and your family. It's important that you have strong faith to go forward.'

Dave Cooke

'Gill stood by me and supported me steadily as our world crumbled around us. She could easily have said, "You've blown everything" but she didn't. She backed me the whole way.'

Dave Cooke

Dave and Gill Cooke

Dave's Mum and Dad dress up as school children to show how to fill a shoe box

'I couldn't do this unless it was for my wife and family. They support me 100 per cent. Gill would be the first to tell me if the work was affecting our family life.'

Dave Cooke

Source of Strength - Operation Christmas Child Days

By the time Operation Christmas Child began, Dave had found his feet again. He had built a house for the family, in Wrexham, where they still live today and was Contracts Manager of a double-glazing business. The first few months were hectic as he divided his time between Operation Christmas Child projects and a full-time job. A typical day involved getting up at 6 a.m., organising the six staff who worked with him before driving to the Operation Christmas Child warehouse, where he split his time between the charity work and his regular employment. Dai would call round and see him every day with an update on how things were going and in the evening Dave would start again, either speaking for Operation Christmas Child or selling double glazing. 'In between, I'd have a mad half hour with my kids,' he said.

From the outset Gill had been completely supportive of the work, although four young children took up most of her time. The children loved going down to Operation Christmas Child after school and working in the warehouse. Gill also looked after the books for their business when Dave later started on his own, and the accounts for Operation Christmas Child. This stability and support meant that Dave was free to get on with establishing the work of Operation Christmas Child, both at home and abroad. Gill and the eldest children have each taken part in Operation Christmas Child trips, experiencing first-hand the work that Dave has given himself to.

The importance of being surrounded by a loving and supportive family, and in sharing life together, has been driven home to Dave only too clearly in his work with Operation Christmas Child. As he travels to different countries, time and again he sees whole villages that have been deprived of fathers and sons killed through war, and children who have never been hugged in their lives. It is a reminder of what a privilege it is to have experienced such love and support from his own family.

Naomi, Simon, Gill, Laura, Dave and Sarah (From left to right)

Simon Cooke in Gakova, 1999

Naomi Cooke in Gumri, Armenia, 1997

Sarah and Laura Cooke

Laura Cooke filling shoe boxes

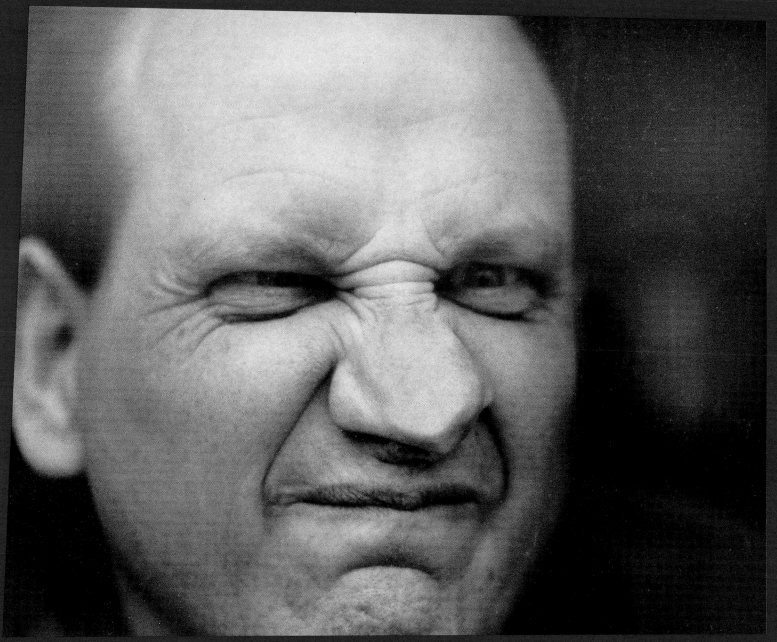

'Dave is an amazing, loveable guy, full of spontaneity and fun.'

David Applin, UK Executive Director of Samaritan's Purse International

57

Love is not just for Christmas

When the first trip was over Dave knew this was just the beginning. A little part of him was left behind in Romania and he was eager to return. 'The mission was on,' he recalls. 'It was no flash in the pan; we knew we were going to have to quickly form a charity and start the ball rolling.' Over the next decade Operation Christmas Child did just that. Becoming something of a national institution among children across the country, Operation Christmas Child continued to grow, and eventually joined up with the more established charity, Samaritan's Purse International. All sorts of ingenious ideas were hatched - some successful, others quickly discarded, but each aimed at bringing a smile to the faces of children who had been robbed of love, homes, family, security, and happiness.

The power of a shoe box

'You get a child to take an empty shoe box, decorate it in colourful Christmas paper and fill it with items like your mum used to do for a Christmas stocking - colouring book, toothpaste, sweets, little toys, hat & scarf. They include a photograph of themselves and a letter - that makes it a personalised gift - and £2 to cover transport, distribution and other related costs. Then we check all the boxes, seal them, and take them abroad. Anyone can make a shoe box. It's not beyond anyone.'

Dave Cooke explains the shoe box campaign

'Operation Christmas Child has become a part of the festive season in the lead-up to Christmas. Children are busy packing their gifts and it also forms a part of the curriculum.'

Ruth Jones,
Samaritan's Purse

It may not look like much in itself, but the power of a shoe box should not be underestimated. It has the unique ability to break through barriers, to spark happiness and excitement, and to bring real joy to those who both give and receive. Probably the biggest Christmas gift programme in the world, the shoe box campaign has been a marvellous expression of love to thousands of suffering children.

Christmas is the celebration of the Father God's love for everyone in the world. Two thousand years ago He sent His precious Son, Jesus, to live among the poor and the neglected. Eventually he died a criminal's death, in order to take the punishment we deserve for ignoring God and going our own way.

Jesus is right at the heart of God's amazing plan to reunite us with Him. All we have to do is receive this free gift. When we do this we can look forward to being with Him forever, free from all the suffering, fighting, disasters, separation and fear that ruin our world.

The shoe box offers a little bit of hope to those in a hope-less situation, and in this sense is a symbol of God's unlimited and unconditional love for us.

'I've had elderly people overseas ask, "Dave, can I have a shoe box please? It's not for me, but I haven't been able to give a gift to my grandchildren for six years. I just want to give them a present." One lady came to me and said, "I just want to hold the shoe box. I'll give it back, but I haven't held anything like this."'

Dave Cooke

'I cannot find the words to describe the impact that these shoe boxes have when they are opened by children who have nothing.'

Rick Parry, Chief Executive, Liverpool FC

Honduras

Nagorno-Karabakh, Armenia

'Shoe boxes can be put together by anyone - they are of limited size. Every shoe box is unique, and goes to another unique child.'

David Applin, UK Executive Director, Samaritan's Purse International

'One school teacher told me she'd lost a week's sleep prior to the distribution, so excited was she that her children were going to receive shoe boxes.'

Dave Cooke

'The Songs of Praise programme was such a great opportunity and elevated Operation Christmas Child onto another level. People throughout the country started sitting up and taking notice. It was incredible.'

Dave Cooke

Songs of Praise

Through the wonders of technology, the BBC organised a live Songs of Praise link-up between St Giles Church in Wrexham and the Second Baptist Church in Oradea, Romania.

On Sunday 12 December 1993 viewers throughout the UK were moved to see the incredible work that Operation Christmas Child does, not only at Christmas, but throughout the year too.

Presented by Pam Rhodes in Wrexham and Alan Titchmarsh in Oradea, viewers were able to see the unity that the shoe box campaign fosters, as they sang and shared in the Christmas spirit together.

The programme made a significant impact and many people who watched were moved by it. As a result, Operation Christmas Child was elevated from a North Wales and Northern England campaign and launched nationwide. 'What we need is lots of little Wrexhams around the country,' Dave said on the programme, and as a result of the Songs of Praise publicity that was just what happened - the profile was raised and people from different regions began offering to become area representatives.

Shoe boxes are loaded onto the 'Big Plane' at Liverpool Airport

Dave Cooke at the controls of the Antonov

The wing span of the Russian built Antonov 124 is wider than a football pitch. It can carry 90 people and more than 120 tonnes of cargo.

The 'Big Plane' & HeavyLift

A major development that was key to the expansion of Christmas Child was the introduction of the 'big planes'. The use of cargo aircraft has not only increased the quantity of shoe boxes that can be delivered but also added a further PR dimension to the charity, with each airlift attracting media coverage and substantial local support.

Three years after the start of Operation Christmas Child, Dave was driving back from Albania with Mark Swindley, known fondly within Operation Christmas Child as 'Rigger'. A pick-up at Heathrow Airport cargo department was scheduled and it gave Dave the idea of using planes in the distribution programme. A large aircraft sitting on the runway with an 'H' on the tail caught his eye. He asked around to see if anyone knew anything about HeavyLift - the organisation behind the big 'H'. He was handed a business card and found himself before long at their headquarters at Stansted Airport, meeting with Director, Graham Pearce, and Vince Jones, a loadmaster for HeavyLift. It was his first encounter with the massive Antonov cargo planes, previously used to carry Russian weapons. They discussed how HeavyLift and Operation Christmas Child could work together to use these enormous planes to deliver aid to areas torn apart by war and disaster. Graham Pearce was captivated by the programme and personally took it on board. The very first airlift was with a Hercules plane but since then the Antonov has been used a number of times each year.

Five HeavyLift planes prepare to deliver a total of 325,000 shoe boxes

When Santa came to Colwyn Bay Conservative Club in North Wales, children turned the tables and gave him gifts to pass on to the Operation Christmas Child Bosnia appeal.

UK Response

Many people see need in the world but are wary about giving to charity because much of their donation may be spent on staffing and administration costs. When you give a shoe box you know that everything in it will reach someone who really needs it.

The campaign has the extra bonus of not just asking children to give money to charity and think they've done their bit. Instead, when children fill a shoe box they experience what it is like to give something of their own to brighten another child's life. At the same time they learn about people who live in a different part of the world.

'Children have discovered that giving gifts can be as much fun as receiving; Operation Christmas Child is as much a part of the Christmas tradition as the school nativity play or a turkey dinner.'

Emma Griffiths, Samaritan's Purse

Housewife Debbie Hurley from Crosby read about the 1993 Bosnia appeal in the Daily Post. She encouraged her family to group together to make a dozen or so boxes but by the time the big plane took off from Liverpool she had accumulated around 1,000! 'It just snowballed,' recalled Debbie. 'So many people wanted to get involved. I even had to ask a shoe manufacturer if they could donate some boxes because I was running out!'

All wrapped up for Christmas!

The wonder of the first trip, back in December, had not worn off by the next Easter. In one orphanage, a boy recognised Dave Cooke and ran across the yard clutching a shoe box under his arm. Written on the top was 'Love from Gareth Owen of Wrexham'. The box was empty, but months later the box was intact, and was a treasure to this little lad.

Operation Easter Child

Operation Christmas Child soon became an all-year programme. The organisers were aware of the many needs in Eastern Europe and keen not to restrict their input to the Christmas season. One of the first steps towards this came in the form of Operation Easter Child with another send off, this time from the Theatr Clwyd on 7 April 1993.

Carefully packed into the convoy were 10,000 Easter eggs, boxes of biscuits, 40,000 specially packed sausages, and 500 pyjamas sewn by local volunteers in their spare time. Other donations included washing machines, cookers, clothes dryers, bathroom and building materials and ten ex-Post Office bikes.

Dai Hughes led the team of 17 who took the supplies to orphanages in the Romanian town of Cluj and the surrounding area. Between six and seven hundred families were touched by the Operation Easter Child and it established Operation Christmas Child as a non-seasonal campaign.

Operation Christmas Child Shop

In October 1993 Operation Christmas Child began a new venture at its birthplace when it opened a shop in Wrexham town centre. Wrexham Maelor Council and local businesses helped with the set up by providing equipment for free. Since the opening, the shop has been run entirely by volunteers. It also serves as a collecting point for emergency supplies such as clothes and food stuffs from rice, pasta, flour and sugar to cooking oil and baby food.

Dave Cooke

Soccer Programme

The dedication to children stretches far beyond delivering humanitarian aid: it's about reshaping fractured lives, moving beyond material needs of the children and giving them the fun and enjoyment of life they have been starved of. The Soccer Programme is right at the heart of the work and has brought summers of fun not only to the children of Armenia, Azerbaijan, Belarus, Bosnia and Georgia, but also to the teams who teach and play with the children.

'I remember lying in bed one night and thinking about the vast number of kids we weren't reaching. I wanted to do something so they could play again.

Whenever we were stuck on borders the guards always wanted to talk about football - Bobby Charlton, Liverpool and Manchester United were part of the international language! And I just wondered if we could do something to communicate with these kids through the world of football.

There's that story from one of the world wars, where on Christmas Day the Allies and the Germans played football together (I think the Germans even won that one too!). Football crosses all political barriers, and that's what sparked off the idea for a soccer training programme.'

Dave Cooke

'The medium of top football is a great leveller. Anyone can take part in the game, and as clubs we have a responsibility to use our power and privileges in a positive way.'

Rick Parry, Chief Executive, Liverpool FC

Dave enlisted the help of the then Director of the Premier League Rick Parry (now Chief Executive of Liverpool FC) who gave his support to the soccer project. Dave was also introduced to former Liverpool winger Brian Hall, who worked as the club's Commercial Manager and was able to organise sponsorship for the project, by way of Liverpool FC strips, souvenirs, footballs and even some of their own coaches.

Bill Bygroves, Pastor & Liverpool FC coach

'Bill Bygroves is a man with a big heart for kids, who communicates through the language of football. He is always ready with a wise word and a supportive prayer.'

Dave Cooke

A far cry from the stadiums of Liverpool and Manchester, the children involved in the soccer project kick their way to victory on pitches in bombed out areas and former minefields.

In these areas of real devastation the little children who have queued up to receive coaching are divided into two groups. Those with bare feet go to grass wasteland that will be softer on their feet, and those with boots or shoes play on hard surfaces.

On one occasion Dave noticed one boy leaning on the goalposts with his boots underneath his arm. Dave went over to him and asked if he was playing, and if he wanted to go over to the hard playing area with his boots. The boy sheepishly turned over his boots to reveal that they had no soles. He just carried them for street cred. 'These are the kind of children Samaritan's Purse reaches out to,' Dave shared. 'They've been forgotten by the adults who are busy rebuilding their own lives. The kids are the ones who really suffer because they're just left on their own.'

'Liverpool FC have been our number one supporter of the soccer programme which, as a Manchester United fan, I find difficult to admit!'

Dave Cooke

Brian Parkinson coaches football in Armenia

'It's great for the adults to see the happiness in the kids faces too. A 40-year-old man in Armenia said to me, "It's been the greatest day of our lives. Thanks for taking time out to come and play with our children."'

Dave Cooke

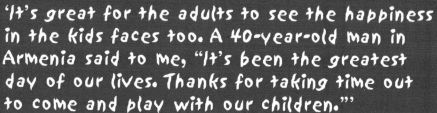

Dave Cooke in goals

The Soccer Programme in action

'At one school in a rough area of Chester the headmaster said to me, "See that girl in the corner. I can't control her throughout the year, but whenever I bring the shoe box programme in it transforms the classroom. The kids just get on with it - watch her now." She put the lid on her box, stood back and looked at it. She kept staring at the box, thinking about it. And then she took the lid off the box and took her own little silver necklace from round her neck. She was a poor kid, but she laid it on the top. To me that was like the Bible story of the widow's mite. It summed it up. Giving to the full. That's the difference a shoe box makes.'

Dave Cooke

Schools

For Dave Cooke, one of the most thrilling parts of Operation Christmas Child has been watching the involvement of children in Britain grow. It's heartbreaking for him to see how much we have in comparison with so many children in the world. 'I often look at what my children have and I struggle with comparing that with what some little ones I meet get by with.'

One seven-year-old boy in Georgia told Dave: 'I wanted to die. I had nothing in my life, but this present told me somebody cares about me. Thank you.' The impact on those who receive shoe boxes and other aid is incredible - but so is the positive influence it can have on the children who give the presents.

Those involved with Operation Christmas Child have been touched by seeing children in this country who care. It's not just the lives of children in suffering countries that are changed, as many teachers up and down the length of Britain can testify.

'I remember a tough little lad coming along with his shoe box. He'd been asked to load shoe boxes into the van I was driving. He came up to me and asked, "Where's it going, mister?" So I told him, and he replied, "When you give this box out mister, to one of those kids, you tell 'em it's from Ryan." It was quite something to see that tough little nut concerned that his box was going to another kid who was not getting anything that Christmas.'

Dave Cooke

I am a shoe box

I am the world's most travelled shoe box! I started my life as a tree. It was a very boring life. I was just standing there in the middle of a forest. But, one year, big men with chainsaws came. It was really scary. The next thing I know, I am an A4 piece of paper, being drawn on by a toddler. The toddler's parents recycled me. I was a newspaper. I told a grandfather of the way tomatoes were annoying Tony Blair and the tragedies of Romania. After three years of recycling and re-forming, I became a shoe box. Suddenly, a child with a familiar face walked into the shoe shop. It was the toddler who had drawn on me years earlier. He bought my shoes and took me home. For six months I lay at the foot of his bed, gathering dust. Finally, I was wrapped up in fancy paper and toys were put inside me. I lay in a school for two weeks before I was put in a van which took me to a plane. The plane then took me to Romania where there were all the troubles mentioned when I had been a newspaper. I was given to a small sad girl. She looked ill compared to the people I knew. She suddenly grinned when I was passed down to her. She opened me up and saw the toys. Now I lie in the corner of a home which is filled with happiness. I am now the happiest shoe box in the world. Perhaps I am the one you sent.

Ben Tickle, Forefield Junior School, Chester

80

Dear Dave,

Thankyou for coming to our class assembly. We hope you enjoyed it. The story you told us about the little boy who wanted an airaplain, was very sad.

When we grow up, we want to do the same job as you. We sent a shoebox to a girl and boy and there was lots of nice things in it.

We hope the little girl and boy like their toys. and hope you have a lovely Christmas and a happy new year.

Love from,
James Grimes and
Katy smith

P.S We think that you are a very kind man and very kind hearted.

Together we can
make a difference

> '**Samaritan's Purse is a big organisation that has opened the world to us, but we still have the feel of Operation Christmas Child.**'
>
> Dave Cooke

'Let my heart be broken with the things that break the heart of God.' So wrote Dr Bob Pierce after witnessing the plight of suffering children on the Korean island of Kojedo. This impassioned prayer led him to found the Samaritan's Purse organisation in 1970 in the United States, with its mission to provide spiritual and physical aid to hurting people around the world.

Over the past 30 years, Samaritan's Purse has helped meet the needs of people who are victims of war, poverty, natural disasters, disease and famine, with the purpose of sharing God's love through his son, Jesus Christ.

'We are an international organisation with a British board and strong links with the American office and the worldwide team of Samaritan's Purse. That's what makes us different.'

David Applin

The vision of Samaritan's Purse ®

After explaining the parable of the Good Samaritan to his followers, Jesus told them to go and do the same thing - and that's exactly what Samaritan's Purse aims to do. Its workers travel the world's highways, looking for victims along the way. The work is often dangerous - as it was for the Samaritan - but the message they carry is much too important. They are quick to bandage the wounds they see, but the Samaritan didn't stop there. In addition to meeting their immediate, emergency needs, they help these victims recover and get back on their feet. As well as help, they offer hope to suffering people in a broken world and share the news of the only source of true peace -Jesus Christ.

WORKING IN THE MIDST OF WORLD TRAGEDY 1979 SAMARITAN'S PURSE AND WORLD MEDICAL MISSION RESPONDED TO THE REFUGEE CRISIS IN SOUTH-EAST ASIA WITH EMERGENCY SUPPLIES AND MEDICAL TEAMS. **1988** SAMARITAN'S PURSE AND WORLD MEDICAL MISSION BEGAN SENDING TEAMS OF DOCTORS TO HONDURAS TO TREAT WOUNDED SOLDIERS DURING THE NICARAGUAN CIVIL WAR. **1989** SAMARITAN'S PURSE BEGAN A PROGRAMME TO TRAIN A CHAPLAINCY CORPS FOR THE CONTRA ARMY. **1990** SAMARITAN'S PURSE PROVIDED 100 MOBILE HOMES FOR FAMILIES DEVASTATED BY HURRICANE HUGO. **1992** SAMARITAN'S PURSE SENT SEVERAL MILLION DOLLARS OF AID TO THE WAR-RAVAGED BALKANS, INCLUDING THE PROVISION OF A 72-BED FIELD HOSPITAL. **1994** SAMARITAN'S PURSE AND WORLD MEDICAL MISSION MOVED INTO RWANDA DURING THE CIVIL WAR TO AID REFUGEES. AFTER THE CONFLICT, THE NEW GOVERNMENT ASKED SAMARITAN'S PURSE TO REOPEN AND RUN THE CAPITAL'S HOSPITAL. **1997** SAMARITAN'S PURSE OPENED RACHEL'S HOUSE IN CONSTANTA, ROMANIA, TO CARE FOR TEN CHILDREN WHO ARE DYING WITH AIDS. **1998** HURRICANE MITCH TORE THROUGH CENTRAL AMERICA, AND SAMARITAN'S PURSE RESPONDED WITH FOOD, SHELTER, MEDICAL TEAMS, AND A CONSTRUCTION EFFORT WHICH EVENTUALLY BUILT THOUSANDS OF CONCRETE-BLOCK HOMES FOR AFFECTED FAMILIES. **1999** SAMARITAN'S PURSE BUILT AND RAN A CAMP IN ALBANIA FOR KOSOVAN REFUGEES. WHEN THE FIGHTING CEASED AND REFUGEES RETURNED HOME, SAMARITAN'S PURSE REBUILT HOMES, SCHOOLS, AND A HOSPITAL IN SOUTHERN KOSOVO.

Dave Cooke with Sean Campbell,
Canadian Director of Samaritan's Purse

'It's not about individuals. Growth doesn't work like that. One man can't do everything; he must be part of a team. My primary concern is to expand God's work. The burden put on my heart was to reach out to children and I have to go about this in the best way possible.'

Dave Cooke

One of the major new stages in the development of Operation Christmas Child was the link-up with Samaritan's Purse International. Operation Christmas Child had got off to a fantastic start, but it was a small organisation with limited experience and resources. The need for an injection of expertise which could take the vision, and in particular the shoe box campaign, to its full potential was an increasing concern.

Enter Sean Campbell of the Canadian office of Samaritan's Purse, the relief organisation headed up by Franklin Graham. Sean saw the vision of Operation Christmas Child and realised the power of the shoe box and its huge potential with the backing of Samaritan's Purse. The timing was just right. The Operation Christmas Child team was all too aware that such a partnership was necessary if they were to take the venture to another level, and merging with Samaritan's Purse seemed to be a perfect solution.

Samaritan's Purse International, had been set up in 1989 by the late George Hoffman as the British arm of the worldwide relief organisation Samaritan's Purse. George, who had previously founded Tear Fund, was killed tragically in a car accident and the Revd David Applin was appointed UK Director in 1995.

Later that year Samaritan's Purse merged with Operation Christmas Child. By then Operation Christmas Child had been offering practical hands-on relief work, primarily to children in Eastern Europe, for over five years. Despite building its own orphanage and delivering nearly a million shoe box gifts in that period, Operation Christmas Child was limited in what it could achieve because it was a relatively young charity with a small but enthusiastic team of supporters.

'We believe a marriage of the two organisations will better serve the cause of both, but more importantly, the cause of needy children throughout the world.'

Dave Cooke, 1995

Franklin Graham gives out shoe boxes in Former Yugoslavia

'Operation Christmas Child has been a relay from the start. I can't claim it's my project. My job was to get the race started and pass the baton on. The vision had to be shared to allow it to grow.'

Dave Cooke

Through contact made in the former Yugoslavia, Samaritan's Purse and Operation Christmas Child had already been working closely together and it was obvious that the two charities had common goals. They both gave practical help to suffering people with the aim of showing God's love in action. A merger would mean that Samaritan's Purse could give Operation Christmas Child the benefit of its 20 years' expertise in relief aid and a more secure future.

In July 1995 this co-operation was formalised with the official merger of the two organisations, with David Applin as Director of the UK operation Samaritan's Purse International and Dave Cooke the Overseas Projects Manager. Operation Christmas Child remains the name used for the shoe box appeal.

The amalgamation of these two organisations has allowed them to share a unique blend of vision and expertise. Samaritan's Purse and Operation Christmas Child project offer direct practical help to their partners overseas, working in difficult and often dangerous situations. By building relationships and maintaining close links with local people in the countries in which they work, they ensure the aid gets where it is needed most and are continually informed of changing situations and pressing needs.

Since the merger of the two charities, the organisation has gone from strength to strength.

- An average of two trucks per month of aid are sent throughout the year from its three permanent warehouses in Loughton in Essex, Eastleigh in Hampshire and Wrexham.

- The charity is on call to respond to emergencies as soon as they occur. They were among the first charities to reach Kosovo during the human tragedy that unfolded there in 1999 and recently were active in El Salvador and India helping the earthquake victims.

- In 2000 a total of 727,606 shoe boxes were sent from Samaritan's Purse-Operation Christmas Child in the UK, with over four million sent from Samaritan's Purse all over the world.

Samaritan's Purse Disaster Relief Unit

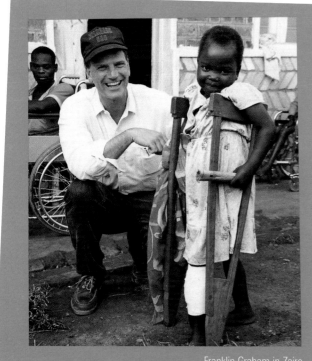

'I believe the joining of Samaritan's Purse and Operation Christmas Child is a tremendous way to reach thousands more children - from the children of Chernobyl to the orphans of Rwanda.'

Franklin Graham

Profile of Franklin Graham

William Franklin Graham III was the fourth of five children born to the evangelist Billy Graham and his wife Ruth Bell Graham. At the age of twenty two, after a period of rebellion and world travel, Franklin committed himself to Jesus Christ while alone in a hotel room in Jerusalem. Soon after that he was invited by Dr Bob Pierce on a six-week mission to Asia. During that time he realised he should commit his life to work with hurting people in areas of the world affected by war, famine, disease and natural disasters. His mission is clear: 'I've been called to the slums of the streets and the ditches of the world.'

In 1978 Franklin was asked to set up and run the medical work of Samaritan's Purse - World Medical Mission - which supplies hospitals and clinics across the globe with the resources they need. The following year he was elected President and Chairman of the Board of Samaritan's Purse, following the death of Bob Pierce after a long battle with leukaemia.

Since then, offices have been established in Canada, Holland, Australia, Germany and in the UK - each office having its own unique identity and character but working together to increase their effectiveness overseas.

Franklin has led the organisation in following the example of the biblical Good Samaritan through more than 20 years of earthquakes, hurricanes, wars, and famine across the globe and the ministry has seen explosive growth. Last year, Samaritan's Purse reached more than 115 countries with nearly £170 million in direct aid.

Dave Cooke and Franklin Graham in Albania

Profile of David Applin

Back in 1992, Revd David Applin thought he was 'retiring' from overseas work and returning to 'a quiet parish life'. But the Samaritan's Purse organisation had other ideas and, after a three-year stint on the UK board, he was persuaded to take over as UK Executive Director: 'I had been involved with the overseas church since 1972 and had been to most parts of the world with Tear Fund. I had thought it was time to stop running around on airplanes and go back to a quiet parish life - but I realised the need was there.'

Ordained in the Anglican Church in 1963, David had been involved with overseas work for the majority of his ministry. After working with the Rwanda Mission in east Africa for ten years he became Overseas Director at Tear Fund, which focused on relieving poverty and suffering throughout the world.

'For me, the uniqueness of Samaritan's Purse is the co-operation between the different offices across the world and its ability to respond quickly. Under the direction of Franklin Graham the organisation is willing to invest time in getting people to meet and develop friendship and understanding. That to me is key. So if there is an urgent need in East Timor, for example, all the offices put into the pot and the Australian office is able to respond - if they don't have much money, then we all put in. A lot of agencies have to raise their own funding and resources for the area they are working in directly but we are able to pull finances and resources this way.'

'Often when an organisation wants to work somewhere they need to talk about it for two years and make major decisions at international conferences, but the American method and Franklin's leadership means we are able to respond as quickly as we can. If something huge happened today we could all say in a few hours what we could do.'

'The strength of the shoe box appeal is that it can be taken on by anybody - a local community, a school or an individual.'

David Applin

'It was clear to me that both organisations could learn much from each other. The 25 years of experience that Samaritan's Purse has accumulated in providing emergency relief around the world is a considerable benefit.'

Revd David Applin, UK Executive Director, Samaritan's Purse International

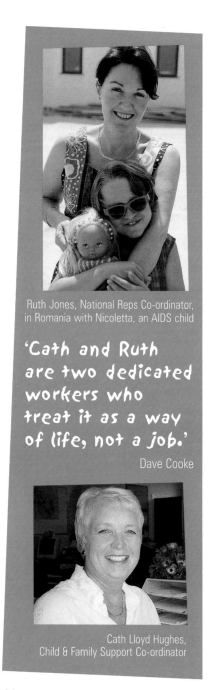

Ruth Jones, National Reps Co-ordinator, in Romania with Nicoletta, an AIDS child

'Cath and Ruth are two dedicated workers who treat it as a way of life, not a job.'

Dave Cooke

Cath Lloyd Hughes, Child & Family Support Co-ordinator

The charity now has an established network of representatives and warehouses mobilising the projects throughout the country. Each year staff from the Samaritan's Purse offices in Essex and North Wales join with supporters of Operation Christmas Child and the team of hundreds of area representatives for a national conference. Reports of the past year and plans for the coming campaign are made, and it's a time to get to know others who have given something of their lives to help children around the world through the work of Operation Christmas Child.

Mary Clements, Area Representative

The very first area representative for Operation Christmas Child was Mary Clements from Sherston in the Cotswolds.

'We are indebted to volunteers like Mary. We couldn't function without these people who give us their time and energy for free. A big thank you to all of them!'

Dave Cooke

'Working with Operation Christmas Child has been totally life-changing, not only for me, but for my wife and children too. I dread to think where I'd be personally without Operation Christmas Child and, obviously, the man who started it. I never thought I'd ever be in a position to help other people in the way I do.'

Mimo Muia, Transport Manager

'I have never heard anyone criticise Mimo, either here or overseas –
maybe that is because he delivers the goods! What he doesn't know about
transport isn't worth knowing. He is a genius with transport logistics and
a very faithful guy.'

Dave Cooke

'Mimo is one of those larger than life characters who has become a very close friend. He has firm values and it takes a while to get into his trust, but once you are there he will never let you down.'

Dave Cooke

The Parable of the Good Samaritan

Jesus said: 'A man was going down from Jerusalem to Jericho, when he fell into the hands of robbers. They stripped him of his clothes, beat him and went away, leaving him half-dead. A priest happened to be going down the same road, and when he saw the man, he passed by on the other side. So too, a Levite, when he came to the place and saw him, passed by on the other side. But a Samaritan, as he travelled, came where the man was; and when he saw him, he took pity on him. He went to him and bandaged his wounds, pouring on oil and wine. Then he put the man on his own donkey, brought him to an inn and took care of him. The next day he took out two silver coins and gave them to the innkeeper. "Look after him," he said, "and when I return, I will reimburse you for any extra expense you may have."

'Which of these three do you think was a neighbour to the man who fell into the hands of robbers?' The expert in the law replied, 'The one who had mercy on him.' Jesus told him, 'Go and do likewise.'

Luke 10:30-37

Crossing borders, crossing barriers

Operation Christmas Child makes up around fifty per cent of the Samaritan's Purse work worldwide - usually slightly more in the UK. But it is not a stand-alone operation and ties in with the Samaritan's Purse aim to meet need any time and any place. As David Applin explained: 'When we see situations through the shoe box distribution we can follow them up through the year. It works very well as a way in but it is not the end of the story. It highlights the need for food, homes, hospitals, medication and equipment that we can go back and respond to.'

Eastern Europe

From the outset, Dave's heart was for the people of the former East European bloc. His contact with the Romanian orphanages had opened his eyes to the needs of many other children: to villages and to whole races that were suffering in different ways just a couple of thousand miles away from Britain.

It is on this region of the world that Dave has focused most of his energies. His desire has been to motivate his own nation to think of the struggles that others are facing both at Christmas and throughout the rest of the year.

'What kind of adults will they be, these millions of children who have been traumatised by mass violence, who have been denied the opportunity to develop normally in mind and body, who have been deprived of parents, of family and community, of identity and security, of schooling and stability? What scars will they carry forward into their own adult lives, and what kind of contribution will they be making to their societies in 15 or 20 years from now?'

Unicef, The State of the World's Children, 1995

Operation Christmas Child operates a no-red-tape response to areas affected by war, famine, disease and other crises.

Albania

Like so many Eastern bloc countries, Albania has been plagued with serious economic problems since the collapse of Communism. The population stands at around three million, but all land is state owned and the high level of government control restricts the economic development of the country. In 1996 public dissatisfaction with the government erupted into civil unrest. Internal difficulties within the country have only been worsened by the flood of Kosovan refugees who have poured over the mountain borders. Dave Cooke first visited the country in the early days of Operation Christmas Child with a truck full of supplies. He has since been involved in keeping a steady stream of humanitarian aid going into the country.

Operation Christmas Child's contact in Albania, Gesina Blaauw, has been in the country since the days of Enver Hoxha. She has witnessed many changes - many, sadly, not necessarily for the better. While it was almost unheard of five years ago, today prostitution is rife. Young girls marry into apparently legitimate Western families only for them to be sent to work as prostitutes when the ceremony is over. The availability of drugs has increased, mostly from Italy, and many addicts are found among the street children.

103

'It was categorised as the second most dangerous place on earth by the year end, and we could see why.'

Dave Cooke

Having responded to an urgent plea for food, Dave arrived in Albania with a truckload of much-needed relief supplies. Their destination was Barum Curri, a border town that was home to the headquarters of the Kosovan Liberation Army. Once in the country, Dave Cooke and photographer, Jonti Wilde, piled into a tiny four-wheel drive for a hair-raising eight-hour journey. All the trees along the route had been cut down to be burnt and sold, and without their roots to hold the earth together the roads were eroding.

'It was like the Wild West - real bandit country. Even in the restaurants the meat was like shoe leather!'

Dave Cooke

Dave and Jonti didn't question for one moment the claim that it was one of the most dangerous regions of the world. Barum Curri was a town obviously dominated by drugs and gun-running. Dave's first impression of the country was one of utter lawlessness. 'Anarchy rules,' he reported at the time. It was in this situation that Dave and Jonti were able to work alongside organisations such as the UNHCR (United Nations High Commissioner for Refugees) and Medecins Sans Frontieres (Doctors Without Borders) to distribute food to the masses of refugees. Much of the work was undertaken from 'base camp' - a large tent well equipped with water and supplies. Situated in a dip in the mountains, it was hidden from the view of the enemy and was the first point of relative safety that fleeing people reached.

The collapse of Communism has increased openness in Albania, but at one point the regime was so strict that there were only two known Christians in the country. The Samaritan's Purse contact, Gesina, was one of them. She is a small yet very powerful lady who is the driving force behind much of the aid distribution in the area and is a wonderful advocate for her own faith in Jesus Christ.

On one visit, Dave met a man in the International Church, who had fallen out of a fourth-storey window and lost the use of his legs. The state provides very little for the disabled, but Gesina met him and provided him with a wheelchair. As he realised that Gesina's love and concern stemmed from her relationship with God, he too made a commitment to trust in and follow Jesus Christ.

Incredibly, when Dave and Jonti arrived in the country and called on a Dutch nurse who was to accompany them to Barum Curri, Dave recognised her immediately! It was Deneke van Veulwen who had worked with Dave's sister, Rachel, in Romania, and so she was already familiar with the work of Samaritan's Purse.

While in Barum Curri, the three of them paid a visit to a farmhouse. It is typical for Dave and others to meet with families to help assess the situation, but on this occasion, it really was a miracle they were there. In this tiny twelve ft. sq. room, one of the family members was nursing a two-year-old baby. While they were there he went into convulsions and stopped breathing. Deneke was able to attend to the child as they rushed him to a medical centre in their vehicle. A saline drip was inserted and the child injected. 'It is difficult to imagine what might have happened had we not been there,' reflects Dave. 'These people have suffered enough.' Four hours later they returned to the farm and the family threw a party to celebrate. The family bought a bag of sweets and passed a bottle of orange juice around. They couldn't afford glasses for everyone, but all everyone was thinking about was that the baby's life had been saved.

Hamallaj Refugee Camp

'I would say that Albania is the poorest country in which I have worked, and not long after the country had opened up we took a convoy of trucks in. My co-driver was Mark Swindley, whose nickname is "Big Rigger". He stands at six feet four and when they saw us get out of the cab the Albanians called us giants because they are quite small!

'We were taken straight to a heavily-guarded compound where, under armed guard, we did daily distributions. In the evening we would play football against our guards. They would stick their Kalashnikovs in the ground to make goals and we would always win because we had a secret weapon in Rigger.

'One evening a guard asked us if we would like to go to his home and we agreed. The home was a little concrete bunker at the edge of the compound. It had no lighting inside - in fact no colour at all. We sat on boxes and were given pink juice to drink. I don't know to this day what it was, but I'm still alive to tell the story!

'The family consisted of Mum, Dad, Granny and two little children, so the next day we made up a food parcel with some toiletries for Mum and toys for the kids and thought no more about it. When we came to move on, a guard came running out waving his gun as we were leaving the compound gates. It was the man who had taken us into his house a few nights before. On a plate he had half a chicken and two tomatoes, which he insisted on us having.

'This would have been his food for his family for a month. I have to ask myself how I would react if I was in their shoes - this man was giving everything'

Dave Cooke

Kosovan refugee children

Armenia

The Armenians have a long history of suffering, perhaps only surpassed by the Jews. Armenia was the first nation to accept Christianity as its state religion, back in AD 301, but since then has endured great persecution and hardship. A number of mass genocides, the denial of a homeland for hundreds of years and the strain of Communist rule has marked its history. In more recent years there has been a devastating earthquake, and an on-going war with Azerbaijan. Collectively, these have devestated families, created thousands of refugees, and strangled the country economically.

The Samaritan's Purse link with Armenia began when Baroness Caroline Cox made a phone call to Dave Cooke. His first response was, 'Who is Baroness Cox?' He was soon to find out more about this incredible woman who has made the most of her position in the House of Lords to reach out to suffering people around the world. One of her main areas of interest is Nagorno-Karabakh.

Baroness Cox offered to fund a visit to Nagorno-Karabakh and Dave agreed to make the trip with photographer Jonti Wilde. The flight to Yerevan, the capital of Armenia, was an unforgettable experience. It took four attempts for the Armenian Airlines aircraft to be loaded and when they were eventually seated, it was next to a crate of chickens! Safety and hygiene were hardly a consideration and luggage was even crammed into the tiny toilet. Dave recalled: 'People were smoking as we went onto the plane, as we took off, throughout the flight - and, of course, when we landed!' Around four hours after take off they were beginning the descent into Yerevan.

'Baroness Cox has done an incredible work out there. They love her - she's even called "The Queen of Karabakh"'.

Dave Cooke

The darkness below suggested landing was not imminent, but they were soon to discover that there were no landing lights at the airport and flares were the only guide for the pilot. Notwithstanding the difficulties, they arrived safely and were soon getting to know a country with whom Samaritan's Purse International would be working very closely with in the coming years.

Dave's very first visit to Armenia and Nagorno-Karabakh offered some frightening, unpleasant, and moving experiences that were to convince him this was a place that Samaritan's Purse should provide help by way of time, love, money, aid as well as, the shoe box and soccer programmes.

When Dave and Jonti arrived in Yerevan they found a capital city bereft of gas and running water. It was like turning the clock back 50 years. A 14-hour journey in an old bus on treacherous roads forced them to keep focused on why they were there. Snow blew in through the gaps in the windows as they headed deep into the mountain ranges that sweep towards the eastern border of Armenia. The final leg of the journey was completed by helicopter. Once over Karabakh the men were dropped to the ground. As Dave ran across the land away from the helicopter he heard shouting behind him telling him to stop. It turned out they had landed in a minefield. Fortunately the snow on the ground allowed him to retrace his steps back to safety.

The hotel conditions were horrendous, with no sanitation whatsoever. But each day they would go with Baroness Cox to find children - young lives that had been scarred by suffering, and left with the constant fear of further loss, injury, or even rape. These children touched their hearts deeply and gave Dave the vision for a work in Armenia and Nagorno-Karabakh. Since then thousands of shoe boxes have been delivered to children in this troubled region of the world, the soccer programme has brought fun and physical stimulation to aspiring David Beckhams, and a range of projects have transformed communities. It has been a journey of hope in an utterly hopeless situation.

Refugee children wait to receive a box of love, Yerevan, Armenia

The key contact in Armenia is a big, burly character by the name of Levon Bardakjian who has been in the country since 1994. He is an Armenian himself, but grew up in California. Along with his wife, Sylvia, he left a prosperous business to come with their young family to Yerevan and they have sacrificed many comforts in an attempt to reach out to fellow Armenians in their homeland. Journalist Bill Spencer said of him: 'The Operation Christmas Child programme exactly fits his idea about impacting the Armenian people. He is always busy but this chance to go out to the needy to demonstrate care and love delights him.' He is widely known by government officials, the Armenian Apostolic Church, as well as the people he seeks to serve. The church he is Pastor of has grown from twenty to over a thousand in a matter of a few years. His motivation: 'Only Jesus Christ can change people from within.'

The Lighthouse

Formerly a student hall of residence, The Lighthouse, is a multi-storey refugee centre housing around 8,000 people on the outskirts of Yerevan. Whole families cram into rooms designed for just one person. When Samaritan's Purse International and Levon first visited this centre, the stench from the toilets, grime and rubbish was unbearable. It was over-stretched for space, and the families living there were, not surprisingly, depressed.

Not only have shoe boxes brought Christmas cheer into The Lighthouse, the charity has also been able to support Levon in an ambitious programme to develop the centre. He has begun language classes, arts and crafts lessons, and Sunday schools. The place has been cleaned up and the refugees housed there have taken part in painting the corridors and brightening up their surroundings. It is now fitted with electricity and transformed into a place that has a positive impact on the lives of refugees who make it their home.

Levon Bardakjian

Gumri

Gumri memorial

Three hours north of Yerevan lies the town of Gumri, the epicentre of the earthquake that devastated the area in 1989. In the space of just six seconds 1,800 people lost their lives. Thousands more found their lives in ruins, ravaged by the loss of family members, homes, livelihoods and for some, their healthy bodies. In this depressed town, a memorial to those who died offers a sombre reminder of the tragedy. Gumri hardly needs such prompting though, as much of the city still points to that fateful day. Shells of imposing church buildings and huge piles of fallen boulders dominate the town square. They say the clock at the top of the tower is still stuck at the time of the earthquake. The emotional effects descend to much deeper levels though, and that's where Samaritan's Purse International makes a difference. In conjunction with Levon it has been able to put a team into this town to work with the victims of the earthquake who have lost homes, family and friends. In this town of phenomenally-resilient people, it is able to support Levon and the team as they help people rebuild their lives in dire circumstances.

'There is a sadness in the eyes of the children of Gumri that you can't forget.'

Dave Cooke

Family living in poor conditions in Gumri

'We were in the "Water Tank Village" and I was hanging back from where the shoe boxes were given out, taking it all in I suppose. A little lad came up and stood in front of me. He didn't say anything; he just looked at me.

'Then he reached out and pulled my arm across him and hugged me. He held me there for five seconds or so and let go. And then he ran off. He just wanted someone to love him. This little lad didn't have a shoe box, he just wanted a hug. It has nothing to do with the material bits inside the box, but just that somebody is showing them love. That's the essence of the campaign. The focus is on the boxes, but really it's about love. That small incident was the best bit about working with Operation Christmas Child - it made me realise why I was doing it.'

Roger Lloyd
formerly with Samaritan's Purse

Shahunian Water Tank Village

An abandoned water project is home to hundreds of refugees outside Yerevan, where huge water tanks have been turned into temporary dwellings. These metal shells are boiling hot to touch in the summer and bitterly cold in the winter, but for hundreds of people it is the only shelter they have. Small stoves offer a little heating and double up as cookers. Each home bears photos, or even little shrines, of family members who have been killed in action. The absence of men in this village is incredibly moving. Virtually every family has lost a father or a son. Hundreds of children will grow up there with very little material possessions, and many without a father.

Samaritan's Purse International has played a crucial part in developing this site into a more habitable village. A shower block and a classroom have been part of this programme of educational and creative stimulation. It is hard to overestimate the difference that the expression of love makes to these lives. Dave Cooke holds near celebrity status in the village. As he climbs out of car or van to visit the site, children run up to him, grabbing hold of his leg, shouting 'Mr Cookie', or clutching pictures of football stars, given to them on previous trips. Many water tank homes are dark, colourless places, brightened up only by the sight of a strip of wrapping paper from last year's shoe box or some shiny stickers that were found inside. They are such tiny offerings, but to a small child who has nothing, they mean the world.

Shahunian Water Tank Village

Azerbaijan

Aid was taken to Armenia and Nagorno-Karabakh by Operation Christmas Child for some years before they were able to cross through political barriers and take some Christmas hope to the children of Azerbaijan. Out of a population of eight million people, a staggering one in seven are refugees. Driven out of their homes during the long, bitter war with Armenia. Operation Christmas Child has been able to reach out to thousands of displaced Azeris, now living in disused railway carriages, makeshift huts and crumbling buildings. However, despite the immense suffering these people have faced, Dave was amazed at the positive attitude they displayed.

Initially approached by a prominent businessman from this country to see if Operation Christmas Child would consider bringing shoe boxes to Azerbaijan, Dave led a team from Samaritan's Purse in the summer of 2000 to run a soccer programme.

A meeting with Azerbaijan's Prime Minister, Gasanov, opened the door to a shoe box distribution in the December of that year. 'What impressed the Prime Minister was the simplicity of the idea: the fact that children are giving gifts from the heart, to other children, without any political or economic motivation.'

'Even though they have been refugees for seven years, they are still full of hope and actually believe they will be going home this year.'

Dave Cooke

'I would like to thank the children of the United Kingdom for bringing hope to our children. One only has to look at their faces to see what it means to them. This visit will raise awareness of their plight and, as each new generation is born, we will need more and more help in making sure that they grow up without the spectre of poverty hanging over them.'

Mr Makhmood, Azerbaijani Deputy Foreign Minister and Ambassador to the UK

Refugees living in disused railway carriages

'I would like to express my sincere gratitude to Samaritan's Purse for initiating such an important activity for the impoverished families of Azerbaijan. The value of such gifts to the children, whose daily life has been that of hardship during the many years of displacement, cannot be over-estimated.

'I would also like to extend my sincere appreciation of the efforts made by the people of the UK to collect those presents and also to thank them for the understanding of the situation in this country.'

Extract from letter from Didier Laye,
UN High Commission for Refugees, Azerbaijan,
15 December 2000

'It is hard to believe that these people have been living in such awful conditions for years. Something is wrong when, at the start of the twenty-first century, children are living as refugees and not knowing whether they will eat that day.'

Dave Cooke

Belarus

Six million people were directly affected by the Chernobyl disaster, suffering from the fall-out of the radioactive cloud that covered the northern hemisphere. Nuclear experts calculate that the explosion released 200 times the radiation of Hiroshima and Nagasaki combined and predict the effects will be felt for hundreds of years.

Perhaps one of the most disturbing situations that Operation Christmas Child has encountered was the orphanage in Blon, Belarus. Housing 60-80 children up to the age of four who had been seriously affected and maimed by the Chernobyl nuclear disaster, it was a desperately bleak institution. In the words of one team member, it amounted to 'one step up from a cattle shed'. These young lives have little hope for the future, many suffering from radiation-related illnesses or terrible deformities.

In 1991 Operation Christmas Child's Dai Hughes and lorry driver, Steve Phennah, made the 1,600 mile journey from Wrexham to Blon where they discovered a scene of devastation that had been hidden from the world. Having experienced the horrors of the first trip to Romania just the previous year, it was unthinkable that Dai was about to walk into something even more disturbing.

Phil Hughes joined Operation Christmas Child on a visit to Blon in the spring of 1995, and recalled: 'One little boy, Valeri, aged five, was back to front from his waist down and couldn't walk. I never once saw him smile until we threw a rugby ball to him and he threw it back.'

Two large lorries had made their way across Europe to deliver an abundance of medicines, food, plumbing materials, clothing, toys, and even a bouncy castle for the children to enjoy.

Unusual play equipment was part of the package of happiness sent from Wrexham to the children of Chernobyl. International food packaging company, Tetra Pak, donated a 'Tetra Castle' made of Tectan, a board made from shredded and bonded cartons, in the hope that it might bring some smiles to the faces of the Belarusian orphans. A delivery of 14,000 Tetra Pak litre cartons of long-life milk accompanied the giant toy - a real godsend as this key nutritional drink was scarce in Blon.

Through an interpreter, one of the nurses, Nina, shared her story with the team. She had worked at Blon for 20 years, first in the sanatorium for TB patients, then with children who had been rejected by their parents and signed over to the state. 'Nina feels ashamed,' explained the interpreter. 'They are all embarrassed that you should see the conditions here. But they are glad you came to help.'

The work at Blon has involved the ongoing process of rebuilding and refurbishing the run-down orphanage. The building has a long history, but poor upkeep over the years resulted in its dilapidated state. Built as an exceptional country gentleman's residence, it became a sanatorium after the 1916 Russian Revolution. At the turn of the eighties, demand for orphan housing was such that it became a home for parentless children. However, it suffered from a lack of resources and fell into a state of disrepair, unable to provide the medical and nutritional attention the children needed. One of the first priorities was to rebuild the collapsing building and install an effective plumbing system. Funds had been so low up until this time that on Sundays the old solid-fuel boiler that heated the water system was left unstoked. In the bitter Russian winters this was no small matter.

Staff at the hospital worked patiently and lovingly, despite the meagre wages. There was no doubt they truly wanted to help the children but hadn't the means to do so. One girl had a cleft palate that could easily be treated in the West. For her though, no such operation was available, and she was desperately underweight because staff couldn't feed her properly. They feared she would die as a result.

'It could take 10 or 15 years before the Government provides the promised new building, so what Operation Christmas Child does we are extremely grateful for.'

Vladimir Razumovski, Hospital Director, 1995

Olya

Dear Friends,

We are writing to you from a small Belarusian village, Blon, which is situated near the city of Borisor, about 100km from Minsk.

We thought that before that we are forgotten by everybody, by God and people, and as if to judge by our salary (£10-15 per month), our government too. There is no school in our village, so we take our children to one 5km from Blon.

But it turned out that somebody in Britain is caring about us.

Several years ago we had guests from Operation Christmas Child. They brought us medicine, food, means of hygiene. They installed very nice bath, shower and toilet equipment and made some cosmetic repair works. We are very grateful and we love them.

With love people from Blon.

One four-year-old girl named Olya caught the attention of the Operation Christmas Child team. During their stay they played with her, and tried to bring a smile to her face. Born without legs, she spent her days propped up on a bench and stared vacantly ahead of her. Her silence was eerie. 'It was as if she knew,' remembers Operation Christmas Child's Ruth Jones. 'The expression on her face was so worldly wise.'

'The children call us "Mama" but they have never known what a true mother is.'

Zoya Baty, Nurse

A cry from my heart

Why is it always the children who suffer?
Why do these little ones seem not to matter?
The kids of Blon are of such tender age,
Doesn't it fill you with anger and rage
That these children are seemingly just cast aside
On the whim of a government trying to hide?

Why, O God have you let this happen?
Why is the graveyard full of these children?
You told us you were a God of love.
But how can you look on these kids from above
And see their hurt and the pain in their eyes,
And do nothing, just sit there as cold as ice.

Why don't you do something? Why don't you care?
Why is life for these kids so unfair?
They don't deserve it, what have they done
To bring all this suffering down upon them?
Please can you answer, if only in part,
Please respond to this cry from my heart.

God's response

If you could see the tears in my eyes
When I see the pain in these little ones lives.
If you could see just how much it hurts
To see my creation being dragged through the dirt.
If my mind could be opened and my heart laid bare
You'd know for yourself just how much I care.

The pain in this world was not by design.
I made this world perfect, it would have been fine
If man had not sinned, and carried on sinning.
'Tis man that has brought about all this suff'ring.

The communist state said, 'There is no God'
So don't be surprised if they ride rough-shod
Over all my compassion, all of my care
And bring about almost unending despair.

But enough of the past, what about now?
I say I am helping - you ask me how?
O why can't you see what it is that I do?
I choose to work through people like you.

That's why people travel for 2,000 miles,
That's why the staff have always a smile,
That's why the little that you can do
Can make such a difference - 'cause I'm in it with you.

Mark Barnes, Operation Christmas Child, 1994

Crimea

Elena

'What impressed me about Elena was the way she related to the kids. Although she wore a nice fur coat, she was never afraid to go down in the sewers and get on her knees to be alongside these kids.'

Dave Cooke

Following in the footsteps of Florence Nightingale, Dàve Cooke found himself in the small country that juts out into the Black Sea, known as the Crimea. This piece of land has been the centre of various conflicts throughout its history. Today it stands as a devastated country in complete chaos. Many teachers have not been paid for months, cars are few because the people cannot afford them and the infrastructure has been obliterated. Yet it is a beautiful country populated by a wonderful people.

Dave made his first visit to the Crimea with Operation Christmas Child to make a video about the street children. Out of a population of over 700,000 there are around 1,500 registered street children. Some of these poor children made their home in the sewers. They would often be high on glue and involved in fighting, even trying to kill each other. It was a desperate discovery, but Dave was there to show them that somebody cared, despite all this; that children back in the UK had sent their love via a simple shoe box. These street kids have very little to look forward to. If they need anything they have to find it for themselves, so to receive a Christmas gift without begging, stealing or searching makes a world of difference in these little lives.

Working alongside a lady called Elena, Samaritan's Purse International has since bought a house for street children in the capital, Simferopol, and begun feeding programmes. There are tremendous needs in this country, and at the moment they are just touching the surface. However, sometimes the smallest of gestures go a long way to make a big difference, as some street children found out on a visit to McDonald's...

'The best $80 or so I have spent in this kind of work.'

'What amazed me was that the lads went in four feet tall, but came out feeling six feet tall. It must have been one of the best things for building self-esteem that I have ever experienced.'

Dave Cooke

McDonalds had recently arrived in Simferopol. It was a star attraction in the city, but the place was empty. The harsh reality was that the people could hardly afford to buy food from the local stores, let alone eat at McDonalds. So Dave had an idea. Wouldn't it be wonderful to take 40 children and the staff who look after them out for a meal? Dave went to the centre for street kids run by Elena and put it to her: 'How would you like me to take all your children to McDonalds?' She said it was the only opportunity they'd ever have to go and broke the news to the children that afternoon.

Dave couldn't pick up all the reactions, but Dave's interpreter Nikolai relayed some of what the children were saying. The boys began to shave their heads so they would be neat and tidy, and the girls were trying on the one dress they had between them to see who would look best in it. The excitement was incredible. Nikolai kept telling Dave, 'If only you could hear everything they are saying!' The boys were asking 'What's a Big Mac?' and 'What kind of food is it?'

Five o'clock couldn't come around quick enough for most of them, but eventually the time came for them to pile into taxis, or buses, or walk to the restaurant and experience hamburgers for the very first time! 'They looked a bedraggled bunch; the boys did anyway - the girls had made an effort to try and dress themselves up,' Dave recalled.

McDonalds issued each child with their meal and various goodies, and they were delighted. Even the centre staff were thrilled with their Happy Meals and balloons. As Dave said, 'We just take these things for granted.' The children were so excited by the experience and were eager to tell everyone about their evening out. Some of the older boys were too proud to take a balloon at first, but once they were home they wanted the balloons and Happy Meal hats - it was all too much to resist, even for the sake of their image! It was an evening the children, staff and Dave will never forget.

Dave's attention was drawn to three children who were sitting on the street together. He took them to a café and presented them each with a shoe box. Through a translator they began to talk. It turned out that two of them were brothers. Dave asked them what they wanted out of life. One of them said, 'I want to be an electrician.' His brother said, 'I want to be a bus driver.' But the other little lad answered, 'I just want to be me.'

A visit to the local authorities to find out about their shelter for street children was on the agenda, which is where Dave met an incredible lady called Elena. She was the director of a drop-in centre for the children. Her ability to communicate with these children, whatever their age, made an impact on Dave. Each child knew Elena by name, and some were as young as three or four. On the streets, with no parents to look after them, Elena played a special role in their lives.

Dave and Nikolai feeding street children

Living in the sewers

Dave's interpreter during his time in Blon was a man called Nikolai. A man of integrity and a stickler for detail, Samaritan's Purse forged a link with him and he has become Dave's right-hand man in Russian speaking countries. It is thanks to Nikolai that Dave is able to operate without treading on toes, as he gives advice on protocol and cultural issues. Dave and he have become great friends as well as colleagues. Speaking of the effectiveness of Nikolai's work, Dave said, 'Quite frankly, we couldn't operate without him.'

Dagestan

'It's a land of astonishing contrasts. You either eat eggs or caviar; you drink either water or champagne.'

Dave Cooke

Imagine flying into Dagestan lying on the top of thousands of cans of food! That's just what Dave Cooke and friends did just after the world had welcomed in the new millennium.

Samaritan's Purse International had been approached about taking aid to the war zone on the Chechen border. This troubled country is home to an amazing mix of people who speak a staggering 35 languages.

Heinz had supplied vast numbers of cans to give out and with the help of HeavyLift, the team loaded the food into the plane, then climbed on top of it and caught some sleep en route to the capital, Makhachkala.

As they emerged from the plane the following day, the bureaucracy held them for hours as passports were checked, the plane inspected, and paperwork filled out. But as they stood on the airstrip, bitter winds swirling round them, a moving scene unfolded. Helicopter gunships were swooping down from the mountains ahead of them. And out of them stepped young conscripts, barely adults, carrying their own friends in body bags.

'We must have seen 50 body bags. It was tragic, these young kids were just being used as cannon fodder. Many of these young men would be haunted forever by their experiences, through no fault of their own. It's bad enough what the Chechens do to their own men when they're deserters, let alone what they do to these youngsters when they get hold of them.'

Dave Cooke

It had been incredibly frustrating to fly into Dagestan, loaded with food to distribute, only to find the process halted by bureaucracy. The team was losing patience, but Dave recalls that seeing the body bags, had a real calming influence on them: 'It put the whole job in perspective to see this waste, total waste of life, right in front of us.'

Eventually they were released and began the two-hour drive up into the mountains. In this country that has been wrecked by war, snow covered the ground and wild dogs roamed the streets where raw sewage ran freely. Armed guards offered 24-hour surveillance, men with huge Kalashnikovs poised ready for action.

Their destination was the border village of Novalask, about a mile from the front line, where the tons of aid were delivered. They were only in the country for 48 hours, but it was an emotionally and physically draining experience. By night, the shelling created an enormous firework display in the sky, something the villagers were by now well used to, but the Samaritan's Purse team had to keep encouraging each other to maintain a level of perspective.

The brief visit to Dagestan was certainly an eye-opener, and one that, despite all the problems, convinced Samaritan's Purse of the need to continue to send in supplies, even if the state made things difficult.

'We couldn't get over the amount of kids that had fingers missing, or ears missing.

'These kids had been held hostage and parts of their body had been sent through the post by the Chechens to get money for guns. It was a lot to take in - to see that this really does happen.'

Dave Cooke

The Balkans

Child standing beside Cluster Bomb

'Our attitude is that if your name is on one of those bullets, well so be it, because we believe that God has a time and his time is right. That's the way we feel about going to these dangerous places.'

Dave Cooke

The troubled region of the Balkans has been littered with tragedies over the past decade, torn to pieces through a complex web of hatred and rivalry. The repercussions will continue for many years to come.

Political sensitivities have been such that officials have prevented Dave Cooke from entering certain regions because he has worked in 'enemy territory', but Samaritan's Purse does not take sides: it aims to serve people whoever and wherever they are in need. The work is often dangerous, and many of the situations are new to Samaritan's Purse. They have to take it one step at a time, helping anyone in need where they can.

'We pride ourselves in being the only organisation to get into besieged Mostar when not even the United Nations could get in.'

Dave Cooke

In the early days of the war in Bosnia, a cartoon was published by the United Nations which mocked Operation Christmas Child. The artist had drawn a teddy bear tied to a parachute being dropped into a war zone. Just a few weeks later the UN were asking Operation Christmas Child for shoe boxes to take into orphanages to bring down barriers.

'It will take a long time for a generation to grow up with a new mentality.
Unless we can teach our kids to love and forgive we've no chance.'

'The children in Kosovo have seen so many things that no human should ever have to see. They have forgotten how to play and smile. Our hope is that the shoe boxes will go some way to easing their pain.'

Dave Cooke

Vladimir and Dusanka Dobric in Serbia were just one couple who experienced first-hand the devastating effects of war. They sent this letter back to the family from whom they received a shoe box:

'After the tragic experience we lived through, our family, composed of seven members, found refuge in Yugoslavia. A good family offered us refuge, they gave us a small apartment. The journey from the town - made on tractor without food or water - lasted for 11 days, through the Serbian Republic. We now depend on the Red Cross.

'Daniel is our little boy and is full of joy and happiness. He doesn't know he has lost his toys and home. He was very happy when he received the parcel you sent him. It is very nice that in this world there are still good people who have hearts for these little ones the war made poor.'

Operation Christmas Child often finds itself in the unique position of mixing with the highest ranks of society as well as the downtrodden suffering masses. This was certainly the case in Serbia, where it was royalty that paved the way for Samaritan's Purse International to help thousands of refugees and suffering families. Princess Kristina of Serbia personally invited them to deliver aid, and they were delighted to accept the invitation. As Dave explained: 'We don't have a political agenda. It is not our business to take sides, but simply to work with anyone who is suffering or in need. We are thrilled when we are able to cross political boundaries to reach out to kids.'

One small refugee whispered in the ear of a Samaritan's Purse worker, 'Please come back for Christmas.'

In a marvellous reversal of roles, Kosovan refugee children living in the Guilden Sutton area of Chester joined in the shoe box campaign in 1999. Kutim Sopa (10), Arlinda Mijuka (8), Adriana Statovici (5), and Leutrim Mjuka (9) helped prepare Christmas presents for their friends back in war-torn Eastern Europe.

'A young girl had interpreted for me a few times. On one trip I met her and this 16-year-old girl told me she'd got married. She was so excited and wanted me to come and meet her husband. We went to their home - literally a six-foot square room with a mattress on the floor. I was given an orange crate to sit on, but you would have thought she was living in a palace she was so happy.'

Dave Cooke

Despite the nature of their visits, it is never guaranteed that Samaritan's Purse will receive a warm reception, as Dave found out on one occasion on the Serbian border. The convoy was flagged down by guards, who informed them that they were suspected of spying. Their bags were opened and the guards found Dave's tiny Ixsus camera, alongside a KGB card he had bought as a souvenir and drawings of a project they were working on. The guards put all the material together and built up a case, resulting in the men being locked in a room on the Hungarian-Serbian border. Amazingly, it was a Samaritan's Purse publicity brochure that saved them. As they were marched into a room and the items placed on the table, Dave was struggling to get them to understand the situation. Fortunately, he remembered the brochure and was able to point out photos of him with the children - proof that he was in fact a charity worker and not a spy!

'Our partners in Serbia, Danny & Vera Kuranji, are an amazing couple. Danny is very cautious in moving forward, and Vera is more the "up and at it" type - a real live-wire. They make a great team, both with an incredible burden for the people in Novi Sad.'

Dave Cooke

Mostar, Bosnia. Black = dead; white = missing

145

Romania

Rachel Cooke in Constanta, Romania

Rachel Cooke with young AIDS victim,
Constanta 1993

The people of Romania have always had a special place in the heart of Operation Christmas Child. It was the destination of their first trip and the work in the country has gone from strength to strength. It has also been very much a family affair for the Cookes.

As Operation Christmas Child has developed, so the projects have diversified. In its willingness to be flexible to meet the real needs of people, Operation Christmas Child has found itself building homes and playparks, organising soccer training, distributing aid and shoe boxes, and sponsoring individuals.

'God's given you the qualifications, so go out there and use them!'

Dave Cooke to his sister, Rachel

At the time of Dave's first trip to Romania, his younger sister Rachel was just completing her nursing training at Great Ormond Street Hospital. She had saved up a substantial amount of money and was looking forward to splashing out on a holiday once she qualified - but God had very different plans!

Rachel had already been challenged to do something to help suffering children through an appeal at her church to fill boxes for families on the Hungarian border. Then Dave returned with countless stories of the horrors of the 'orphanages' and hospitals in Romania, and put it to her straight: 'God's given you the qualifications, so go out there and use them!'

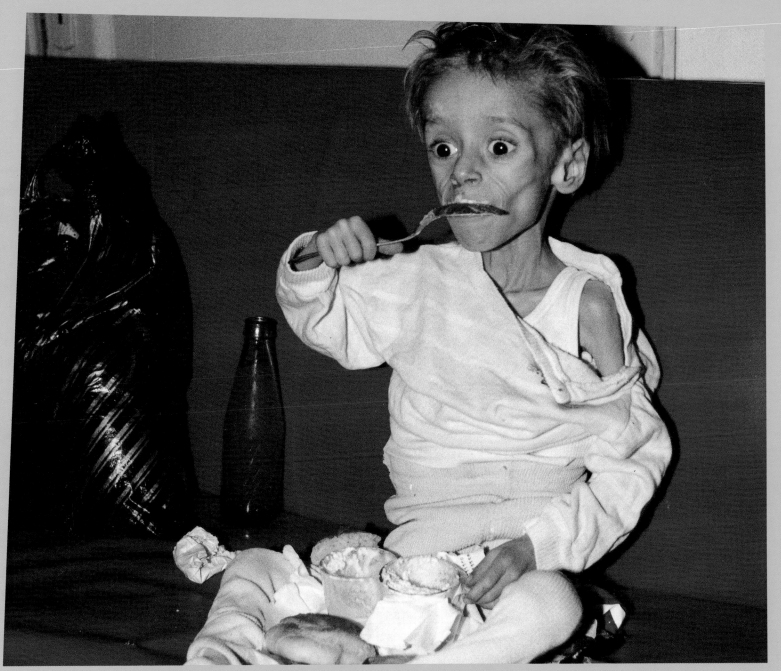

A young child with AIDS, close to death

'I always wanted to be married with a big family, and I think God has a sense of humour in this one! A real driving force in my life has been the 300 or so kids I've looked after and to whom I've been able to show love and respect in both life and death.'

Rachel Cooke

So it was that, instead of soaking up the sun in an exotic location, in the summer of 1991 Rachel somewhat reluctantly began work in the Infectious Diseases Hospital in Constanta, Romania. It was a stark contrast to the famous Great Ormond Street Hospital. She was now working with little or no equipment, drugs, nutritious food or even nappies. However, she did have a God-given love for these children and a gift of caring for and nurturing them.

In the early days, Laing Homes had helped Operation Christmas Child build a family group home for orphans in Cluj, Romania, called 'God's Mountain'. It wasn't long before Rachel recognised that these abandoned HIV/AIDS children needed a similar family environment where they would be given love and care for the duration of their short lives.

Fundraising for such a home began, and Laing Homes came on board again as the chief sponsor, offering their planning and building expertise, and donating all the equipment and supplies. Volunteers made their way over to Romania and set to work, building and preparing 'Rachel's House' ready to welcome its first children.

'It was priceless to see the joy and happiness on the faces of these children who were at least going to have a home and be loved for the duration of their short lives.'

Dave Cooke

It wasn't all straightforward. As one staff member explained: 'When they first moved into the house we thought love and patience would turn them into confident children right away. But we didn't know that it would be so hard for them to overcome their early experiences living in an institution, in which their dignity and souls were so badly hurt. At the start they destroyed the furniture, pulled all the curtains from the windows, had the most unexpected reactions and just couldn't cope with so much around them. Even the therapist didn't have any ideas of what to do in certain situations. The time went by with daily new challenges. Love was the key, and love won. All your prayers helped us so much in finding what is right to do.'

Dave Cooke opening God's Mountian, Cluj, Romania

Children enjoy playing at God's Mountian

Ian Mackenzie ('Mackers'), former Project Manager with Samaritan's Purse, who co-ordinated the building of Rachel's House

Rachel's House is currently home to nine children aged between 12 and 13. They attend the local school and have been accepted by the community.

Staff at Rachel's House see the amazing gift of hope that Samaritan's Purse has given to their children and community in the following terms -

- A new life to the children, with real values and the possibility to serve God;

- An opportunity for all the staff to learn so much and to love more;

- An opportunity for the community to see a good example of how to fight for the best values in the world: the love values.

Hearts of Gold

Rachel Cooke was taken completely by surprise when she was awarded a 'Hearts of Gold' award by Esther Rantzen. Rachel thought she was going to speak to a group of student nurses about her work with AIDS babies in Romania, when one 'student' put up her hand and asked a question. She turned out to be Carol Smillie, who revealed the real reason Rachel was there, and led her onto the set of the BBC's 'Hearts of Gold' show to be presented with her award.

'God has given me a fantastic gift of nurturing and it has been a privilege to use it to be mother to hundreds of children.'

Rachel Cooke

Russia

If Dave Cooke had been told back at the time of the Communist regime that one day he would drive a convoy of trucks around Red Square in Moscow, he would have laughed in disbelief. But that was exactly what he found himself doing and it is an experience he will never forget. Samaritan's Purse has worked with an organisation called Compassion Ministries to reach out to the thousands of children living on the streets of Moscow and other Russian cities. Shelters have been built to house children, soup kitchens set up, and money has been poured in to support ongoing work in this former Communist stronghold.

In April 2001 Dave Cooke was awarded the Pushkin Award in recognition of his Humanitarian and Spiritual Care to Young Children in Russia.

Enna Slavishenskaya

Enna Slavishenskaya is another of Samaritan's Purse's partners who has been most effective in guiding Dave through cultural sensitivities. If he needs to make a speech, Enna talks him through the situation, giving him the required level of understanding. In his own words, 'Enna is firepower to the elbow. Like Nikolai in Belarus, Liviu in Romania, Levon in Armenia and Danny and Vera in Serbia, Enna has opened up many doors for us and helped us to be more effective. Plus I love them to bits!'

'Our partners there tell us that one of the major problems is a new generation in Russia raised on the streets without parents, control or hope.'

Emma Griffiths, Samaritan's Purse International

Non-Eastern European Countries

While the main focus of the Samaritan's Purse work in the UK has been on the former Communist Eastern bloc, Dave Cooke and others have visited troubled areas in different parts of the world to deliver much needed aid.

Thailand & Cambodia

Cambodia is most well known for its tragic 'killing fields,' where tens of thousands died at the hands of the infamous Pol Pot. The former prisons, piles of bones, and the killing fields themselves are all preserved as a kind of showcase of horror. It's an eerie place, and one that reminded Dave once again of the mess the world is in. 'It was just frightening to think that one man could control and do all this kind of thing. It was a chilling reminder of man's inhumanity to man.'

Despite the stunning beauty of both Cambodia and Thailand, these countries are rife with prostitution and abuse. Dave Cooke joined a team from the Canadian Office of Samaritan's Purse on a visit to Cambodia to see how they could help children who have been sucked into this desperate system. There are some heroic people working with these girls, setting up projects and trying to rescue them.

One young girl they met was being sold on the streets. When they asked who her father was, she replied that he was the Chief of the Police. Dave found it staggering that anyone, let alone someone so senior in the Police, would sell their daughter.

Rwanda

Operation Christmas Child found itself in a country that was completely chaotic and incredibly dangerous. The plane arrived early and they were very nearly shot out of the sky. When they did eventually land, there was one solitary man standing guard. Not much was left of the airport; bullets and shells covered every wall. The lone guard stood next to a string that went across the road. Dave recalls this almost ridiculous scene: 'I remember a can of coke in the middle of the road with the string just touching it. It was that low. I didn't speak the language, so I just stepped over the string to walk and meet our partners. I didn't really think anything of it. But the guard immediately cocked his rifle. He was ready to shoot me there and then. He literally wanted to show he was in charge of this string hanging across the road. It was totally mindless and reflected much of the country. They needed to show they were in control. I couldn't pass that string until he moved it.'

The sight of tiny children surrounded by their massacred families and neighbours has been one of the most horrific to hit our television screens and newspapers during the past decade. The psychological damage to these children is difficult to comprehend. For this very reason, Operation Christmas Child decided to fly in thousands of shoe boxes - tiny gestures of hope to help in what will be a long and painful healing process. Graham Pearce of HeavyLift stepped in once again and generously supplied the giant Antonov plane to take a total of 65,000 shoe boxes to the children of Rwanda.

'As we drove through the jungle on our way to an orphanage we heard children singing. It made the hairs on the back of my neck stand up. We arrived and met them: hundreds of children who had lost their families. They were sitting in rows and rows, all in the same colour shirts and had shaved heads. They had waited six hours for us, sitting underneath the trees. It was an amazing sight.'

Dave Cooke

The Samaritan's Purse village housed thousands of malnourished Rwandans who sat in groups with shaved heads, mourning the loss of their families. A square of carpet was laid out on the grass where 40 babies were being wet-nursed. They ranged from newborn to two years old. Some of them had even been raped and each one of these orphans had been left to die.

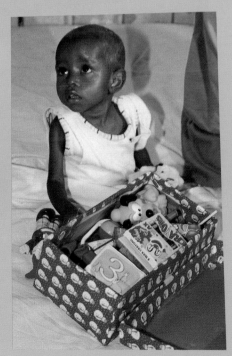

Genocide - the policy of deliberately killing a nationality or ethnic group.

New Collins Dictionary

One little girl was offered an orange. With deliberate hesitation she put her hands out to accept it, but lifting her big brown eyes up to Dave she asked, 'Is it all for me?'

Kigali Hospital

A shoe box distribution in Kigali's hospital was a small flicker of hope to the hundreds of children being cared for there who had witnessed and experienced unthinkable atrocities. Huge chunks of their tiny bodies had been hacked off and were only covered by loose bandages. As shoe boxes were handed out, their eyes opened wide as they eagerly stretched out their little hands to receive their very first present.

'I've seen the devastation caused by war in Bosnia but there can be no comparison to what I've witnessed in Rwanda. It's a small arms war with many of the injuries caused by landmines and machetes. The amount of people missing limbs is shocking.'

Dave Cooke

'You can imagine what it was like. Rows and rows of little orphan children receiving their shoe boxes. It was all noise, and screams and high-pitched squeals!'

Dave Cooke

Big names, big business, big news

'So many people have been involved in Operation Christmas Child - far too many to mention - but each one has been a part of making this happen. We're indebted to lots of amazing people who've given so much to help those with so little.'

Dave Cooke

There are many people who have thrown their weight behind the work of Operation Christmas Child and this can only give a taste of their support. The celebrities who have offered invaluable PR; the journalists who have raised awareness of the plight of children; the businesses and individuals who have reached into their pockets and given so generously to support the projects: this book is a testimony to each one of them.

'I see myself as a modern day variation on Robin Hood - taking from the rich to give to the poor.'

Dave Cooke

'This is how we know what love is: Jesus Christ laid down his life for us. And we ought to lay down our lives for our brothers. If anyone has material possessions and sees his brother in need but has no pity on him, how can the love of God be in him? Dear children, let us not love with words or tongue but with actions and in truth. This then is how we know that we belong to the truth, and how we set our hearts at rest in his presence whenever our hearts condemn us. For God is greater than our hearts, and he knows everything.'

I John 3:16-20

163

Sponsors

'I cannot thank enough those people who have given to Operation Christmas Child. Nothing could have been achieved without them. They too have been a voice for those who cannot speak for themselves.'

Dave Cooke

The worldwide vision of Operation Christmas Child could not have been realised without the generous and faithful financial support of individuals and corporations alike. From the outset, Operation Christmas Child attracted an overwhelming response to appeals for funding. Some of these supporters have stuck with the campaign throughout. Other sponsors discovered the appeal at a later stage - whether through seeing media reports of the campaign, the shoe box collection 'in action' in their local community, or, in one case, through Dave Cooke threatening to spill his breakfast over them!

Janet Rothera & Graham Pearce of HeavyLift with children in Azerbaijan

'HeavyLift have been exceptionally generous towards the cause and we are indebted to them for their contribution.'

Dave Cooke

Britain's leading parcel carrier, Parcelforce, came on board in 1995 and for many years was a vital part of the shoe box operation, supplying vehicles free of charge to help in collection and distribution.

Operation Christmas Child got off to a flying start at the South Woodford branch of the Christian retail group, Wesley Owen Books & Music. The entire chain has served as a drop-off point for Operation Christmas Child. In one branch, manager Dominic Stinchcombe let his creative juices flow and designed a special plane to promote the shoe box campaign.

Thorntons

Children of former Yugoslavia enjoyed a special treat in 1996, when confectionery giant Thorntons donated hundreds of pounds of their famed toffee to Operation Christmas Child.

Reg Vardy

Reg Vardy garages, based in the North East of England have backed the work of Operation Christmas Child in various ways - both seen and unseen. From supplying vehicles to collecting shoe boxes, to encouraging other companies to supply trucks, Reg Vardy has been a friend in need to Operation Christmas Child.

Kwik Fit

Kwik Fit revved up the shoe box campaign, offering their branches as collection points, and encouraging both staff and customers to get into gear and fill a shoe box.

Dave first met one supporter, entrepreneur Geoff Lloyd on an early morning flight. They engaged in small talk as Dave struggled to keep his food from landing in the businessman's lap. Once breakfast was cleared away and the risk of spillage reduced, they began talking properly. 'I remember saying to Geoff, "How would you like to be Father Christmas to thousands of kids?"' Geoff asked how much Dave was looking for. Dave replied, 'Nothing' and handed over their latest promotional video. Two weeks later Geoff arrived at Daves office and agreed to go on the next trip along with his son Roger. The trip made such an impression on Roger that on his return he began working full-time in the Samaritan's Purse office.

Dave Cooke with a van donated by Norweb

Celebrities

The birth of Operation Christmas Child in 1990 could hardly have been more successful from a PR point of view. It managed to capture the local community and make an incredible impact. The power of the media was clear to all, but how could they sustain such a level of interest? The first distribution had been a drop in the ocean and public enthusiasm was vital for continuing to reach out. They quickly realised the role that celebrities could play in this area. The early years saw a steady stream of stars who offered their support, whether by filling a shoe box themselves, making an appearance at the send-off, or actually going on one of the trips. Over the years, Operation Christmas Child has gathered an eclectic mix of famous supporters to whom it is indebted.

Mr T from the TV series 'The A Team' was one of the first stars to do his bit for the campaign. He was in pantomime in Liverpool and agreed to come to a send-off in Wrexham.

The first big send-off from Chester saw a Hercules plane used to wing the shoe boxes to their destination, courtesy of Graham Pearce of HeavyLift. The Alessi Twins from Neighbours were flown up specially for the launch by British Aerospace; Olympic Gold Medallist Cyclist Chris Boardman was also there along with George Harrison's wife, Olivia, and Radio 1 DJ, Simon Bates, who did a live show from the send-off.

Comic actor Norman Wisdom is no stranger to suffering. Not only has he experienced sadness in his own life and family, but he has also spent time in Albania. Under Communism, all Western films were banned - apart from those featuring Norman Wisdom! To many Albanians, he is better known as 'Mr Pipkin' and this has given him a special interest in the country. He was happy to take part in one of the Operation Christmas Child promotional videos to support its work.

Mr T

'Very early on we realised the power of using celebrities for PR purposes. We are aware that they are very busy people, but when they catch the vision it's incredible the influence they can have.'

Dave Cooke

Norman Wisdom

Mark Hughes joined Dave Cooke & Dai Hughes at one of the early Operation Christmas Child send-offs

The Duke of Westminster

For several years the Duke of Westminster has thrown open the doors of his Cheshire home, Eaton Park, to launch the Operation Christmas Child shoe box campaign. He agreed to become a patron of this locally-based charity and has continued to support it over the years.

'The Duke has been a great supporter of the campaign in many ways. We owe so much to him.'

Dave Cooke

David Applin, Dave Cooke & the Duke of Westminster

'We are grateful to the many high-profile individuals who have taken time out of their busy and demanding schedules to lend their support to the cause.'

Dave Cooke

Bishop Michael Baughan

Michael Baughan the former Bishop of Chester, joined David and Dawn Applin on a trip to Bosnia.

His diary, reporting on the suffering and devastation they witnessed was published in a local newspaper. It touched the hearts of many.

Bishop Michael Baughan

The Tribe

A little bit of Manchester made its way over to Azerbaijan in December 2000, when five-piece dance outfit The Tribe joined Dave Cooke and others in distributing shoe boxes. Formerly known as World Wide Message Tribe, the pop-group has sold over a quarter of a million albums - but are not planning to make a fortune or even get famous. Its sole aim is to use music to make the Christian message real and relevant to young people.

Back in Manchester the band's daily routine involves going back to school as a part of the work of The Message Trust, taking lessons, assemblies and lunchtime concerts with a mix of live performance and biblical teaching. It's not the glamorous lifestyle normally associated with a pop-group, but that's what makes them different. That's why they love the work of Operation Christmas Child.

'We can get so comfortable in this God-given life and fall into the Western rat-race. The trip to Azerbaijan gave us a taste of what it is to show unconditional love to another human being - something Jesus knew so much about. It was a real privilege.'

Lindsay West

The Tribe featured on the 2000 promotional video, using their experience in schools to encourage children and young people to take part in this exciting project that reaches out to people of their own age who have so much less than they do.

'It's been a real privilege for The Tribe and The Message Trust to be involved with Operation Christmas Child. Watching the young people at our Planet Life event fill a van with 1,600 shoe boxes and then The Tribe escorting them to Azerbaijan was one of the highlights of the whole year.'

Andy Hawthorne, Director, The Message Trust

'The trip to Azerbaijan - what a rollercoaster ride! On the one hand it was heartbreaking to see the state that people in our world are living in, and on the other it was an amazing privilege to be part of making a difference to many lives.'

Tim Owen

'It was an experience that everyone should go for - it was such a challenge to us who have so much yet still want more. When are we going to be thankful and content with all that God has blessed us with and share that with those who have less or literally nothing?'

Emma Owen

Nia

A young Welsh singer known simply as Nia had made quite a name for herself singing contemporary Christian music both in the UK and in the United States. Dave wondered whether they could put on a roadshow with Nia to raise awareness of the shoe box campaign throughout the country.

As a result, Nia went out with Operation Christmas Child to Armenia. The children there loved listening to her sing, and many joined in, clapping and dancing along to the music. The trip also captured Nia's heart. For the next few years, she went on the road with Operation Christmas Child throughout the UK during the autumn. She would perform in the schools and tell the children about the difference a shoe box can make to a child in Kosovo, or Croatia, or Romania.

'Nia's talents as a singer and performer were just what Operation Christmas Child needed to make a real impact in schools in the UK. She is great at conveying the message to the children, both through her songs and in explaining the vision of the work, in a way that grabs the attention of the children.'

Dave Cooke

Over the years, Operation Christmas Child has gathered an eclectic mix of famous supporters to whom it is indebted.

Olympic Gold Medallist, Jonathan Edwards, supporting the shoe box campaign with his sons

Newcastle United FC

Bobby Robson

175

The Media

Di Ried, Producer of Songs of Praise

Philip Hayton and his crew Steve Hewitt and Nigel Roberts

The power of the media has been apparent throughout the history of Operation Christmas Child, from the television screen that brought Dave Cooke the first images of Romanian orphans to the PR machine of Marcher Sound and the Wrexham Mail that captured the hearts of the local people. The continued support of the media in news items, features and programmes such as Songs of Praise has allowed Operation Christmas Child to become widely known and accepted.

Many talented journalists, photographers, film crews, presenters and producers have offered their time and talents to Operation Christmas Child. Each one of them - again too many to mention individually - has brought their unique style and expertise to the charity, all with the ultimate aim of helping as many children as possible.

Kristen Gurumurphi of Channel 4 was most supportive and went to Bosnia on the Hercules, from which he made a programme on Operation Christmas Child.

Philip Hayton of ITN travelled with Operation Christmas Child on a number of occasions without charging any fees. He has assisted in making and fronting promotional videos, as has former BBC presenter, Jan Leeming.

Granada Television, GMTV and the Welsh Television Networks have been extremely supportive of Operation Christmas Child and have sent excellent film crews on various trips.

'Many people in the media are fairly hardened and cynical about what goes on in the world but, for me, Operation Christmas Child has really touched a raw nerve, because this is practical Christianity in situations where people, certainly from the West, would rather not be.'

Les Lever, journalist.

Les Lever

Captured on Film

'So much of the growth of OCC is down to the impact of poignant pictures. We are indebted to photographers who have given their time and expertise – often free of charge.'

Dave Cooke

There is no doubt that a photograph is worth a thousand words and Operation Christmas Child is indebted to the stream of outstanding photographers who have supported them so ably through this medium.

Jonti Wilde and Dave Cooke share plenty of priceless memories of their many trips together. Jonti's skills with the camera have been used time and again by Operation Christmas Child and in the wider work of Samaritan's Purse.

Steve Hewitt of the BBC has given so much to Operation Christmas Child by offering free of charge, his time and expertise as producer and director for many of the promotional videos. His photographs, and those of Vic Cleavely and Richard Clayton have been invaluable in advancing the cause.

Nigel Dobson's role as photographer and journalist has also been invaluable to Operation Christmas Child, producing pictures and words that speak straight to the heart.

Filming and photographing suffering people is a highly sensitive issue. Paul Davis, who filmed the AIDS babies with whom Rachel Cooke was working, should be commended for his high degree of professionalism and compassion.

Jonti Wilde

Nigel Dobson

Steve Hewitt in Romania

The need
never stops

'Over the years we have discussed how long this would run but, as someone once told me, "Christmas will never go out of fashion." I think Operation Christmas Child has quite a long way to go.'

David Applin

Operation Christmas Child is now enjoying its second decade of existence. During the course of its relatively short history many lives have been changed and whole communities have been transformed. It has brought smiles to the faces of thousands of children. Dave once said, 'You might think I'm crazy, but I firmly believe that lives can be changed through a shoe box.'

'I've been doing this for many years but it is still happening. Millions of refugees are still homeless and living in poverty. It will never cease to amaze me what the human body can endure despite the terrible conditions people find themselves in; they still dig in and continue to hope.'

Dave Cooke

So, what of the future? Suffering is not in decline. What can be done to reach the children and communities that have no lens of hope and love through which to see the world? Dave's answer is straightforward: 'If we are going to influence this world for good, the mindset of people has to be changed.' That's no small task, but Dave insists it is not overwhelming: 'We must start at the beginning, and that's with children. Jesus said, "Let the little children come to me", and that's the programme in its simplicity. Let's not complicate things.'

'We've come a long way since 1990. It's been gradual growth but has been a constant injection of adrenalin!'

Dave Cooke

'We're not scratching the surface yet. We hope to increase it to over one million shoe boxes going from Britain each year, but we need people to keep hold of the vision, not to think it is old hat, but to remember what it's like to give a kid a shoe box who's not going to have anything else at Christmas.'

Dave Cooke

From its inception, Operation Christmas Child has been all about children. Dave acknowledges the existence of poverty, suffering and pain in Britain, but feels it was the children outside of this country that God laid on his heart: 'Definitely my burden - and this isn't the same for everyone - is for the kids abroad, who live in such dire poverty that I can't describe.'

'No child should have to wake up screaming in the night because they've seen their mother raped in front of them, or their father mutilated. No child should have to live on the streets or have to be born in a sewer. I don't see these things in this country, so my burden is for kids abroad, and particularly the former CIS countries.'

Dave Cooke

There is no question that the shoe box was a stroke of genius that has carried Operation Christmas Child from strength to strength. But has it outlived itself? Dave is adamant in his response: 'I don't think we've even had a drop in the ocean yet. The shoe box programme amazes me - it doesn't have a shelf-life! When you give a child a shoe box, they cannot believe it is all for them. Anyone who has seen the effect it has realises and understands that we must continue with it.'

'Bringing a smile to the face of a child devastated by war is the ultimate Christmas present anyone can give.'

Tracy Turton, Derbyshire Times

There is no greater example than Jesus Christ, the most tender-hearted man who ever lived, who gave everything so that we can ultimately be free of all the suffering, heartache, loneliness and pain in the world.

Romanian boy living on a rubbish tip

'It still makes the hair on the back of my neck stand up and breaks me inside to see kids suffering and living without hope and love. The day I stop being affected, if I get blasé or accept what I see, that's when I'll finish. I'll have lost my edge, and you can't do this work without it.'

Dave Cooke

'We're never short of tears on these trips. You feel so helpless, and that's when we pray that the little we do will make a difference.'

Dave Cooke

'In a hundred years from now it won't matter what kind of car I drove, the size of my bank account or what type of house I lived in, but that I was important in the life of a child.'

Anon

Every shoe box touches a child. If someone decides not to take part in the appeal one year then that is one child less who will receive a box. Similarly, if someone decides to take part, then that is one more child who will receive a gift.'

David Applin

Hello my unknown Friend,

I was very happy to get your Christmas gifts. I am 9 years old. I have a small brother who also got presents, and he was very pleased with that. We have not father. After father's death [Nicolai: in civil war 1990 - 1993 in the Northern Georgia] I did not think that I would receive any present from anybody. Because my mother could not find job we are living in very poor conditions. There was chocolate in that box you sent for me. I did not eat chocolate for a long time because of our poverty. And because God looked at me, He sent presents to me, and I got a hope and began to pray in order He send such a person who would help me with treatment for my eyes ... I am losing my eye sight. I have a wish, while I am not blind yet, I could see people who gifted such a joy for me. Because later I will not be able to see them ... I love you very very much. Every night before going to bed I thank God sent such good people to me. While I am writing this letter my smaller brother is staying by me. And he asks I write you that he also loves you. When I received those presents we've been told that Organisation of Uncle Dave Cooke sent those presents to us. And I do ask you to kiss him [Dave] instead of me. I am writing this letter with a pen you sent to me. I kiss you all many many times.

From
Ms Nino Kakhishvili
Telavi, Georgia

You too could
be involved!

For further information about the work of Samaritan's Purse and Operation Christmas Child please contact:

Samaritan's Purse International Ltd
Victoria House
Victoria Road
Buckhurst Hill
Essex IG9 5EX
Tel: 020 8559 2044
Fax: 020 8502 9062
Email: 100067.1226@compuserve.com

Samaritan's Purse
PO Box 3000
Boone, NC 28607
USA
Tel: +828 262 1980
Fax: +828 266 1056
Email: info@samaritan.org

Or visit our website at www.samaritanspurse.org

SAMARITAN'S PURSE®
INTERNATIONAL✝RELIEF